REV UP
ROBOTICS

Real-World Computational
Thinking in the K-8 Classroom

JORGE VALENZUELA

International Society for Technology in Education

PORTLAND, OREGON • ARLINGTON, VIRGINIA

Rev Up Robotics
Real-World Computational Thinking in the K-8 Classroom
Jorge Valenzuela
© 2020 International Society for Technology in Education

Editor: *Emily Reed*
Copy Editor: *JV Bolkan*
Indexer: *Valerie Haynes Perry*
Book Design and Production: *Jeff Puda*
Cover Design: *Edwin Ouellette*

Library of Congress Cataloging-in-Publication Data

Names: Valenzuela, Jorge (Engineering teacher), author.
Title: Rev up robotics : real-world computational thinking in the K-8 classroom / Jorge Valenzuela. Description: First edition. | Portland, Oregon ; Arlington, Virginia : International Society for Technology in Education, [2020] | Includes bibliographical references and index. | Identifiers: LCCN 2019055100 (print) | LCCN 2019055101 (ebook) | ISBN 9781564848178 (paperback) | ISBN 9781564848154 (epub) | ISBN 9781564848147 (mobi) | ISBN 9781564848161 (pdf)
Subjects: LCSH: Robotics—Study and teaching (Elementary) | Thought and thinking—Study and teaching (Elementary)
Classification: LCC TJ211.26 .V35 2020 (print) | LCC TJ211.26 (ebook) | DDC 372.35/8—dc23
LC record available at https://lccn.loc.gov/2019055100
LC ebook record available at https://lccn.loc.gov/2019055101

First Edition

ISBN: 978-1-56484-817-8

Ebook version available.

Printed in the United States of America.

ISTE® is a registered trademark of the International Society for Technology in Education.

About ISTE

The International Society for Technology in Education (ISTE) is a nonprofit organization that works with the global education community to accelerate the use of technology to solve tough problems and inspire innovation. Our worldwide network believes in the potential technology holds to transform teaching and learning.

ISTE sets a bold vision for education transformation through the ISTE Standards, a framework for students, educators, administrators, coaches and computer science educators to rethink education and create innovative learning environments. ISTE hosts the annual ISTE Conference & Expo, one of the world's most influential edtech events. The organization's professional learning offerings include online courses, professional networks, year-round academies, peer-reviewed journals and other publications. ISTE is also the leading publisher of books focused on technology in education. For more information or to become an ISTE member, visit iste. org. Subscribe to ISTE's YouTube channel and connect with ISTE on Twitter, Facebook and LinkedIn.

Other Titles in the *Computational Thinking and Coding Across the Curriculum Series*

No Fear Coding: Computational Thinking Across the K-5 Curriculum (2017), by Heidi Williams

Creative Coding: Lessons and Strategies to Integrate Computer Science Across the 6-8 Curriculum (2018), by Josh Caldwell

Coding + Math: Strengthen K-5 Math Skills With Computer Science (2020), by Nicole Howard & Keith Howard

To see all books available from ISTE, please visit iste.org/resources.

About the Author

Jorge Valenzuela is an adjunct professor at Old Dominion University and the lead coach at Lifelong Learning Defined. He's also a national faculty member for PBLWorks, a published researcher, and an avid blogger, with his work featured in *USA Today*, Mediaplanet USA, Edutopia, ISTE, eSchool News, *Tech & Learning*, PBLWorks, and on Medium. His work helps educators and learners understand and implement computational thinking, computer science, STEM/STEAM, and project based learning. Valenzuela is a recipient of the ISTE Computer Science Excellence Award and STEM Excellence Awards. He also earned the Lynn Barrier Engineering Leadership Award for his contributions to STEM education in the Commonwealth of Virginia.

Acknowledgments

I want to personally thank the following people and entities for being a part of my life and education journey—thus helping me learn many valuable lifelong lessons.

The Creator, for grace and faith; my parents, Anisa and Daniel, for being the BEST kids a guy could ever have; Mariam, for being my perfect life partner; the Valenzuela family, for your unconditional love; the Elizalde and Flores families—we are fortunate to have you all; the entire Roache family—thank you for being a part of my life; the Pratt family; the Douglas family; the Rojas family—I love you; the Shokooree family; the Zambonino family; the Nash family; the Reddington family; and the Katz family.

Ms. Tamu, Rick, and the Best family, Adeel and the Memon family, Shawn Alleyne, Phillip Bristol, the Acosta family, the Ramadan family, the Kyles family, the Jones family, the Holiday family, the Rasheed family, the Brown family, the Jackson family, Zane Robinson, Wanda McLean—you are my sister, and every friend I ever made.

My students—thank you for inspiring me to continuously work on my craft.

The entire ISTE staff and organization and especially to Diana Fingal—thank you for your friendship, mentorship, and for making a difference in my life; Richard Culatta, Joseph South, Heidi Ellis, Camila Gagliolo, Beth Miranda, Boyka Parfitt, Simon Helton, Lauren Kocher, Octavia Abell, the STEM PLN, the CSN PLN, Juli and Joseph Kleinmann, Jessica Shupik, Valerie Witte, and Emily Reed for believing and supporting me in this project every step of the way.

The Commonwealth of Virginia, Senator Tim Kaine, Governor Ralph Northam, Pamela Northam, Dr. Tina Manglicmot, Chuck English, Dr. Janice Underwood, Dr. David Eshelman, Amy Sabarre, Rebecca and Chris Dovi, CodeVA, Timothy Ellis, Dr. Hollee Freeman, and the staff at the MathScience Innovation Center, the STEM Education Commission, the Honorable Atif Qarni, Dr. James Lane, and the Virginia Department of Education for truly ensuring that Virginia is for *all* learners.

The curriculum and instruction and CTE instructional specialists at Richmond Public Schools, Jerry Browder, Dr. Deborah Jewell-Sherman, Dr. Yvonne Brandon, Deborah Kyles, Barbara Smith, Nelson Colbert, Bill James, Darlene Smith, Dr. Ernestine Scott, and Victoria Oakley.

Rody Boonchouy—for giving me my shot, Dr. Gina Olabuenaga—for teaching me how to teach, Bob Lenz, Brandon Wiley, Becky Hausammann, John Larmer, Suzie Boss, Kendall Tripathi-Clark, the entire PBLWorks staff and national faculty—you leave your family and homes to better our schools worldwide and I am so proud to be a part of this team; the Unicorns—I love you all for being a special band of educators who inspire me daily.

Ayah Bdeir, Grace Morales, Christine Leonard, and the entire littleBits staff; lead educators and Bitstars! Dr. William Wright, Tammi Ward, Dee Biggers and the entire staff at Hertford County Public Schools; Katie de la Paz, Steve Barbato, Jenny Buelin and the entire ITEEA staff; Samer Rabadi, Tom Berger, Laura Lee, and the entire editorial team at Edutopia; Dayna Laur, Andrew Miller, Al Summers, Jill Clayton, Chris Woods, Tim Cavey, Michael Cohen, Rae Hughart, Jeff Gargas, Michelle Moore, Chad Anthony Ostrowski, Katelynn Giordano, Dr. Charity Moran, Lacrecia Terrance, Tiffany Ott, Rachelle Poth, Jamie Connally, Aaron Eisberg, Ben Owens, Brian Schoch, Chris Fancher, Drew Hirshon, Erin Gannon, Kris Hanks, James Fester, Jim Bentley, JoAnn Groh, Kelly Reseigh, Kiffany Lychock, Kristen Uliasz, Mike Kaechele, Randi Downs, Ryan Sprott, Teresa Dempsey, Rich Dixon, Tiffany Frierson, Michael Courtney, Marsha Granderson, Kenyatta Lewis-White, Katrina Futrell, Shayla Adams-Stafford, Vicki Davis, Dr. Karen Sanzo, Pitsco Education, Code.org, Project Lead the Way, Sphero Education, Logexsoft Inc., Davina Ruiz, and Michael Niehoff.

Old Dominion University, Dr. Petros Katsioloudis, and the faculty in the STEM Education and Technical Studies academic program.

Contents

PART 1 Planning and Building Student Capacity for Robotics

PART 2 Robotics in the Content Areas

PART **3** Strategies and Approaches for Teaching Robotics and Computational Thinking

Foreword:
Two Perspectives on the Use of Robotics in K–12 Education

Nicholas Provenzano (@thenerdyteacher)
Makerspace Director and Middle School Robotics Coach
University Liggett School, Grosse Pointe Woods, Michigan

Whether they were inspired by Transformers, Voltron, or C-3PO, kids have long dreamed of having their very own robot. In education, the idea of robotics in a school setting was once reserved for colleges and maybe some advanced classes for students in the 12th grade. All of this has changed as technology has progressed to the point that different types of robots are becoming available that can be coded by K–12 students. As a teacher, the idea of bringing a robot into your classroom sounds like a crazy thing to consider, especially if you are not a STEM teacher. As an ELA teacher, I thought the same thing, but I was able to explore many wonderful things thanks to embracing robotics in its many forms.

I was always looking for ways to engage students in writing. Having students write traditional "How to" essays always ended with lots of instructions for making PB&J sandwiches. One day, I was watching my son play with Sphero and littleBits and it clicked that I could have students build or code with these tools and also write out the directions for someone else to recreate in class. I quickly put together a lesson plan, gathered the materials, and had an amazing lesson with very engaged students. I learned that it's not about the tool, but how it can be used to support learning. This concept is why *Rev Up Robotics* is so important for teachers looking to explore robotics and computational thinking.

This book is perfect for educators who know a little about robotics and those who are completely new to the concept. Jorge has broken the book down into several different parts to help someone understand what robotics is in the context of education, and how it can be applied to different curricular areas. By providing actual lesson plans, Jorge supports any educator who picks up the book. On top of the content that is in the book, there are also QR codes that a reader can scan to be taken to even more resources to support their understanding of robotics. The book is not just about robots though, and that is why I like it so much.

Some people just talk about the physical aspect of robotics without really acknowledging the type of thinking that is required to fully embrace robotics as a concept to support learning. Jorge spends time sharing research on the value of computational thinking in the classroom and how it supports learners long term. Giving students problem solving skills in a variety of ways can only help them as they move on in their learning and later as adults. This focus is why the book is an important read for any educator interested in not only implementing robotics in their classroom or school, but supporting stronger problem solving skills through CT. This is the book I will be recommending to any teacher interested in starting their robotics journey.

 Jaime Donally (@JaimeDonally)
Author, speaker, and edtech consultant specializing in
practical use of augmented and virtual reality in the classroom

As my passion for augmented and virtual reality has grown, I've become more aware of the coding skills necessary to prepare for this wave of the future. The skills needed to develop the hardware and software for the trending immersive technology are extremely difficult to find, and companies are constantly searching for skilled developers to bring their big ideas to life. The need continues to grow as the demand for the new technology increases.

In my personal educational experience, I was never exposed to coding instruction, but now it's common to see our classrooms implementing these foundational skills and starting as young as kindergarten. I'm amazed at how quickly our students pick up these new skills and I applaud the companies and movements that have captivated our students with fun and engaging learning. While traditional methods of teaching computer science skills might seem repetetive, boring, or overly technical, we now see students eager to "play" with code.

As a learner, I've always preferred to learn through play. My competitive nature gave me the drive to persevere and solve complicated problems. Many of our students also show a positive response from challenging obstacles, as long as it's paired with guidance and encouragement. The learning environment for coding allows students to make errors, experiment with real-time results, and build confidence in their own skills to create anything they can imagine.

One of the ways we can easily see the programming visualized is in robotics. The use of robotics in education is a powerful way for students to see their work immediately reacting, from writing the code to the response from the robot. Robotics is a way of seeing computer science skills in action, offering a connection and motivating factor for students.

The beauty of this book is the guidance it offers educators with little to no past robotics skills. Valenzuela supports the educator to understand the basics of robotics, the use of robotics including lesson plans and standards, and the pedagogy and cross-curricular teaching strategies for effectively teaching robotics with students from kindergarten to eighth grade. Similar to augmented and virtual reality, the various levels of robotics can range from beginner to advanced. Regardless of where the educator begins, the many resources shared will bring them up to speed and equip them with helpful tools and strategies for teaching with robotics.

As immersive technology, artificial intelligence, and robotics continue to grow within K–12 education, this book will play a vital role to support all educators with the necessary skills to prepare learners for their future.

Dedication

This book is dedicated to every teacher working to develop themselves into the educator that their students need.

Introduction

My Computer Science Story

I first discovered computer science (CS) over 20 years ago while completing my undergraduate work in the Management Information Systems degree program at SUNY Old Westbury in New York. At the time, I wouldn't have predicted that eventually, CS would become the new literacy or that I would be working with others to make these skills accessible for all students. My experiences working in the education field over the last 15 years have taught me that it takes will, know-how, technology tools, practical strategies, and patience to do this work. My experiences have also lead me to believe that the goal of CS for all students can be achieved in many classrooms across various content/program areas by engaging learners experientially in these complex skills through design and inquiry practices.

Personally, I must admit that while in college, I (like many) struggled with the core CS concepts. I needed assistance in mastering computational thinking and the necessary trigonometric functions for programming in C++. Luckily, a friend and mentor, Shawn Alleyne, helped me get grounded in both computer programming/coding principles and see the big picture by connecting my learning to my love of video games and, later, through developing flowcharts for systematic planning. Little did I know that Shawn's techniques would become the cornerstone for my future classroom instruction with students and also with educators who attend my project based learning (PBL), computational thinking (CT), and programming/coding with robotics workshops.

When Shawn began coaching me, I asked him, "If I'm learning about computers, then why am I taking four high-level math courses?" He said, "Jorge, computers are made up of two things: hardware and software. The hardware is anything you can touch. The software is your computer programs on the hard drive. Without software (or apps), the computer will not function." I still didn't understand (it was 1997 and I didn't own a computer). He then asked me, "What do you like to do?" At the time, I hadn't done anything yet, so I said, "play video games!" He said, "Think of the Street Fighter video game. When two of the street fighters are engaged in combat and one attempts to strike the other in the face, either he will block the blow, duck, or get struck in the face. A computer programmer using logic wrote code in a sequence of instructions to make that happen. As the street fighter jumps around the screen and uses other techniques, more complex algorithms within data structures are used to make that happen." Shawn then showed me flowchart representations of basic algorithms. His initial lessons enabled me to learn how both industrial and software engineers (among others) use flowcharts for system or programming design.

That was the first time a teacher ever connected a topic in a school subject to something I was interested in, and in the process contributed to building my foundational knowledge in the governing principles needed for mastery of the skill(s). Shawn's easy to follow lessons made learning programming and CS fun, more accessible, and compelled me to continue developing myself so that one day, I too could help others access this information by teaching them about CS through various edtech tools like robotics and now this book.

Computer Science Becomes Relevant in Schools

Although this book is about educational robotics, it is impossible to set the stage for robotics without mentioning the relevancy of CS in today's schools. After all, several aspects or branches of the CS discipline (such as computer programming and artificial intelligence (AI)) can be taught through robotics. When I began teaching in 2002, there wasn't a CS-related teaching endorsement in my home state of New York. Luckily, when I moved to Virginia in late 2003, the endorsement was available for my teaching license, but there weren't any CS programs in schools that I was aware of. I, therefore, took up the Technology and Engineering Education discipline—which I came to love and support teachers in for nine years during my tenure with Richmond Public Schools. Little did I know that one day CS would be the future of education or that Congress would officially make CS part of STEM by the STEM Education Act of 2015 (Guzdial & Morrison, 2016). A year later, in 2016, President Barack Obama announced the Computer Science for All initiative and then in May of that same year Virginia governor Terry McAuliffe signed legislation mandating that CS, CT, and coding be incorporated into the Virginia Standards of Learning (Llovio, 2016).

In support of Virginia's new policy, many art, career and technical education (CTE), mathematics, and science teachers throughout the Commonwealth now require assistance making this transition. Pioneers of this movement, Rebecca and Chris Dovi of CodeVA (along with others) have been leading the way in providing teachers and schools with both curriculum and professional development in CS. My many travels (25 states and 60 plus cities) have alerted me to the fact that departments of education throughout the country are now beginning to articulate similar mandates for incorporating CS into K–12 instruction. Even the White House has made expanding access to learning CS education a high priority for the current Secretary of Education. This is actually a good thing—a *very* good thing! Not only will learning CS skills through programming, coding, and various edtech tools (like robotics) help teach kids to think computationally, it will also provide them the exploratory and preparatory skills needed for many of today's jobs and careers.

The Inspiration for This Book

First, I would like to acknowledge that the inspiration for my work are the countless educators that I meet in my travels and also online through various collaborations (Twitter, Instagram, and the ISTE Computer Science and STEM networks, among others). Helping address their immediate instructional needs is what primarily guides my research (Valenzuela, 2019) and is the focus of my research agenda and the workshops, podcasts, webinars, journal articles, and how-to blogs that I continuously develop.

With CS now getting such a big push nationwide, I receive many requests from teachers for assistance with understanding components of the K–12 Computer Science Framework, the CSTA standards and the ISTE Standards for Educators. More specifically, many of these educators are wanting to level up their skills for engaging students in robotics by having them build and program robots. Luckily the majority of my undergraduate work was in both CS and business, and I have a degree in Management Information Systems (MIS) from SUNY Old Westbury in New York. I also hold CS teaching credentials in Virginia, which makes it possible for me to help.

Although I don't currently prepare students for a specific CS course, I am conducting my Ph.D. research on employing the right strategies for proper teacher preparation for both CT and CS. The findings in my preliminary data collections, my CS knowledge, and experiences in STEM and PBL enable me to offer targeted assistance to educators from a broad range of content and program areas. Some of these include ELA, math, science, art, and CTE teachers who are interested in teaching CT and CS core concepts and practices in tandem with their core curriculum.

Ever since my days with Richmond Public Schools, robotics has been a popular go-to tool for many of the teachers I've worked with. It all began for me when we used VEX robotics in both our Project Lead the Way engineering classes and after school robotics programs throughout Richmond. We used both VEX and LEGO in our middle school programs as well. I later transitioned into a National Teacher Effectiveness Coach (NTEC) with the International Technology and Engineering Educators Association (ITEEA). There I coached adults in building and programming VEX robots for their engineering design high school classes. To share these vast experiences on a broader scale and with educators everywhere, in 2017, I began creating how-to blogs for ISTE, Edutopia, PBLWorks, littleBits, and Medium. These various writings caught the attention of the editors at ISTE, and with their guidance, I set out to make this book a how-to guide for schools and K-8 educators interested in teaching robotics and real-world computational thinking without having to make too many changes to the focus of their curricular contexts. I hope this book becomes a widely used resource for districts, schools, and enthused educators everywhere to level up their teaching practice with robotics.

Who is This Book for?

This book is written for K-8 teachers who may or may not have some experience with robotics and are looking to incorporate robotics into what they already do but may be unsure of where to start or how to scaffold the learning experiences of their newbie to experienced learners. Through lessons on the fundamentals of computational thinking and programming, and evidence-based teaching strategies, both the novice and expert can level up their use of robotics and have a good foundation for CS by applying the contents in this book. Whether you're a CS, ELA, math, science, history, art, or technology teacher, this book will provide you the know-how for strategically engaging your learners in lessons designed to help them construct and utilize their knowledge about robotics and CS basics effectively. Additionally, this book is also for the teacher who is interested or tasked to hold an OST (out of school time) robotics club or looking to prepare students for competitive events. So, whether you are introducing robotics to students in a lesson, for competitive events, in an after-school club, or just as a fun activity, you will find lessons in this book to support you on your journey of teaching robotics and beyond.

For Content Area Teachers

If you teach one of the core content areas (ELA, mathematics, science, or social studies), you will find a chapter dedicated to aligning important learning goals in your subject with robotics activities. However, this book does a lot more than that. It also provides you the basics and fundamentals of computer science, engineering (STEM), and computational thinking as they pertains to robotics and your content area. The reason for this is because robotics is not just a stand-alone activity. It is an amalgamation of several multidisciplinary skillsets found in various disciplines (among them mechanical engineering, electrical engineering, computer science, and STEM).

The support in this book also extends to assisting you with identifying your content area standards for each robotics activity or lesson as well as the appropriate correlations between them and both the ISTE and CSTA standards. Lastly, examples of how the content in this book is used across multiple classrooms are also highlighted—along with recommendations for the use of sound teaching practices that should be a part of every classroom. Constructivist learning (including project based learning) is also highlighted because the learning theories associated with constructivism inform the majority of the curriculum referenced in the book. It is, therefore, important for teachers wishing to teach robotics to maximize the learning outcomes of students by applying what we know to be sound from the learning sciences.

Elective teachers will also find something useful in this book by using the learning goals in their standards as guidelines. As most standards and competencies already correlate in multiple ways to the four core subjects, simple modifications will easily fit the context of multiple classes.

For Technology and Computer Science Teachers

If you are already teaching robotics, CT, and programming in some form, you will find this book helpful for assisting you with creating cross-curricular connections for your students and perhaps even for your colleagues. Both the computer science and engineering aspects of robotics and programming are currently hot topics in schools. And although many technology classes have covered many of these items in previous years, it is important to effectively convey the relevant and meaningful work we do with our students to our stakeholders. Therefore, highlighting computer science and interdisciplinary learning by adapting many of the lessons in this book, or perhaps in your own lessons, may provide you the opportunity to demonstrate the value of your discipline and course(s) to the K–12 community at large.

How to Navigate and Use This Book

This book is organized into three parts and each part has 3–4 chapters.

Part 1: Building Capacity for Robotics with Foundational Knowledge and Skills (Including Computational Thinking)

This section explores the basics of robotics, the building of robots, how robotics is used in the real-world, and how this context pertains to computer science. Computational thinking is highlighted in this section as a foundational skill necessary for engaging students in more complex tasks with educational robotics.

Part 2: Robotics and Computational Thinking in the Content Areas

This section provides evidence for educational robotics and examples of robotics taught successfully in the classroom. There is a dedicated chapter for each of the four content areas that aligns important learning goals in each discipline with activities that use robots and robotics. This section also provides teachers the basics and fundamentals of computer science, engineering (STEM), and computational thinking as they pertains to robotics and also for elective and after school classes.

Part 3: Strategies and Approaches for Teaching Robotics and Computational Thinking

This section provides teachers examples and recommendations for the use of sound teaching practices. In this regard, constructivist learning (including project based learning) is highlighted so that teachers who teach robotics, computational thinking, and programming can maximize the learning outcomes of students through the learning sciences. This section also shares practical tips for establishing an afterschool competitive robotics club.

Planning and Building Student Capacity for Robotics

This section defines robotics, identifies how robots are used in the real world, and outlines their multiple uses in schools and across the curriculum. The information and resources introduced in this section will help you build a foundation for successfully integrating robotics into your lessons by providing a meaningful learning context, tips for engaging students beyond play and tinkering, and the prerequisite knowledge needed for the activities in parts 2 and 3. The chapters in this section will explore:

- **Creating a plan for robotics**
- **Educational equity and access to robotics tools**
- **Tips for collaborating with colleagues**
- **Computational thinking as a foundational skill for robotics**
- **The basics of building and programming robots**

Robotics:
Introduction and Applications

Robotics is a branch of engineering that involves the conception, design, manufacture, and operation of robots. This field overlaps with electronics, computer science, artificial intelligence, mechatronics, nanotechnology, and bioengineering (Rouse, 2015). In the popular 1941 story, *Liar*, science-fiction author Isaac Asimov first coined the term robotics. Therein, he described Asimov's Three Laws of Robotics, which even today are considered the three guiding principles for how both robots and smart machines should behave.

Asimov's Three Laws of Robotics

1. Robots must never harm human beings.

2. Robots must follow instructions from humans without violating rule 1.

3. Robots must protect themselves without violating the other rules.

Examples of Robots and Their Use

In the real world, robots free humans from repetitive tasks by helping with assembly, welding, handling a variety of tools, heavy labor in space, manufacturing, military missions, car production, surgeries, underwater exploration, and duct cleaning, among others. For making classroom projects with robotics authentic, I have compiled eight uses for robots that I believe teachers can leverage to provide meaningful context for student work.

1. Military Missions

Robots used in the military save lives by performing hazardous tasks and missions that replace human intervention. Explosive Ordinance Disposal (EOD) robots are used in military missions to locate and disable both mines and improvised explosive devices (IEDs) in suspected packages and areas of importance. Air forces also use drones (uncrewed aerial vehicles) in military observation missions to help locate hidden explosives and for broad range surveillance.

2. Commercial Agriculture

Agriculture is the science of cultivating soil for growing crops and rearing animals to provide food, wool, and many other essential products. Robots contribute significantly to the field of commercial agriculture. Similar to their ability to do multiple manufacturing jobs, robots navigate farmland, harvest crops, and care for plants independently. Moreover, the robots used in agriculture can work more efficiently, faster, and longer than human labor.

3. Law Enforcement

A range of very sophisticated remote-controlled robots is used by law enforcement to fight crime and to protect the safety of our public and police officers. Police robots have cameras and infrared lights and are capable of finding precise locations during police missions. A robot commonly used by law enforcement is the Robotex, which is water resistant, agile enough to climb stairs, and has a handy 360° camera for helping officers catch potential perpetrators and suspects.

4. Automotive Services

The automobile industry reduces both manufacturing and labor costs by using robots with powerful mechanical arms, tools, wheels, and sensors for building and car assembly. The automotive industry also employs robots for tasks such as precise installations, sealing, painting, and welding.

5. Artificial Intelligence

Artificial intelligence (AI) is the branch of CS that pertains to the development of computer programs that perform tasks which would otherwise require human intelligence. Today, AI is used in a variety of ways, such as Google searches and the tailored recommendations we find on our Amazon accounts. However, AI is also used to control robots—which makes it possible for intelligent robots (Alexa and Echo, among others) to interact with humans in their homes by helping with household chores, providing security, and entertainment. Extensive strategic and systematic use of artificially intelligent robots (the intersection between robotics and AI) in manufacturing aids in consistency, saves time (robots do not get tired or need breaks), and saves money on labor.

6. Space Exploration

Both the Remotely Operated Vehicle (ROV) and the Remote Manipulator System (RMS) are the two most common robots used in a variety of space missions to provide astronauts the ability to explore. Both robots can capture data and footage that humans would never be able to without their assistance. ROVs have unmanned capabilities and can orbit freely or land on an outer space surface to explore terrain. RMS mechanical arms assist astronauts with performing critical and dangerous tasks during space missions.

7. Mechatronics

Mechatronics refers to the multidisciplinary branch of engineering that deals with engineering mechanical and electrical systems. It also includes the study and intersection of diverse topics such as computer science, systems, robotics, electronics, and telecommunications. A mechatronics engineer understands how to join the principles of mechanics, electronics, and computing to develop better, more cost-effective, and reliable systems. Many secondary and post-secondary institutions dedicate courses of study to mechatronics.

8. Competitive Robotics

During events held all over the world, teams of individuals build and program robots to compete with other robots to determine which was best at accomplishing a task or series of tasks. Many of the teams partaking in competitive robotics are comprised of students in the K-16 setting, but professional competitions are also becoming more common. Many criteria can be used to classify competitions with robots, so there is no standard way of referring to them. Some may include criteria such as the nature of movement, the use of branded materials (such as LEGO or VEX) versus open materials, indoor versus outdoor, and students versus professionals. The final chapter of this book is dedicated to this topic in the context of the K–8 setting.

Robotics in Schools and Teaching with Robotics

Thanks to the nationwide thrust of both STEM and CS, robotics is no longer reserved to factories, after school clubs, or groups of children participating in competitive robotics. More and more K–12 educators want to engage their learners in this fun and academic phenomenon but often are faced with hurdles that cause many of them to retreat. Obstacles include insufficient access and availability, lack of funding, or being unfamiliar with how to make robotics rigorous and aligned to the content being taught.

Luckily for teachers, both the CS and STEM core concepts and practices associated with robotics do not change, but due to the efforts of organizations such as ISTE, Code.org, LEGO, and others, their place in the curriculum has and will continue to do so. That means that more teachers can and should engage their learners in robotics to make this dynamic learning opportunity equitable for all learners.

Robotics is an excellent tool for teaching kids the most fundamental engineering design and programming skills while allowing them to see and interpret the results of their build and program in real time. Furthermore, through building and programming robots, K–8 learners can learn about CS, mechatronics, coding, literacy, physical science, mathematics, planning, healthy competitiveness, teamwork, and perseverance. And because all of these aforementioned items are relevant to knowledge and skills are that are needed by all students to understand and navigate a successful future, I believe this also serves as a fundamental component of equitable education.

Learning robotics and participating in competitive events also helps students understand the use of robots in more authentic contexts, such as those described in the previous section.

Anyone Can Teach Robotics

Teachers with no background or previous experience with robotics often ask if it is possible to teach it to their students. The short answer is yes, provided some prep work is done beforehand. Before introducing new robotics content or any technology tools to students, it is essential to assess your knowledge of the content and skills needed for successful teaching. Once you are set to start, make time for researching, learning, playing, and testing—either on your own or with a colleague. The good news is that you do not have to spend much time on your own to develop the right skills to be effective.

Like most technical fields, computer science requires lifelong learning and often "experts" have to be "beginners" when encountering new material. My advice is to become comfortable with this and to dedicate some time weekly to enhance your knowledge and skills gaps. Our students will not always see the light at the end of the tunnel, and many become discouraged when they do not achieve as well as others or see immediate progress in their skills. It is therefore essential for us to always model what we want to see in them and that includes continuous learning. When educators actively learn alongside their students, the term lifelong learning is unfolded and better defined for young learners!

In the next chapter, I provide the intended learning along with specific strategies that any teacher (expert or novice) can use to introduce robotics to their students in logical steps. The appendix is also outlined similarly (in logical next steps) for developing both your knowledge and skills base at your own pace.

CHAPTER 2

Planning for Robotics:
Set Yourself up for Success

Before diving into educational robotics, educators must ask themselves several key questions that may include some of the following:

- How will incorporating robotics into my instruction meet the academic needs of my students?

- Will I begin by infusing robotics into some of my daily lessons, or as part of an after-school club?

- Do I want to get my students involved in competitive robotics?

My recommendation is to first determine where robotics will live in your curriculum—either as part of the instructional day or in an after-school program. If you're new to this process, make things easier for yourself and create a planning committee. A planning committee will help you determine what you will need to know and do, gain the support of key stakeholders, and build a solid case for robotics at your school.

Planning Steps and Considerations

A planning committee will not be hard to create, but the results you're seeking may not happen overnight. Therefore, with consistency, proper planning, and a pleasant disposition, set out to do your work. To help you get started, here are ten vital steps for creating consensus for robotics at your school in tandem with leveling up your skillsets.

1. Garner the support of your school administration.

2. Create a written plan of how robotics will meet the academic needs of the students.

3. Poll students to gauge their buy-in.

4. Create a list of needed items and a budget.

5. Create a realistic timeline.

6. Find teacher and parent helpers.

7. Determine storage and meeting locations.

8. Keep communication open.

9. Use social media.

10. Improve your own learning gaps.

1. Garner the support of your school administration.

In today's educational climate, most administrators will not have to be sold on the value of infusing robotics into your curriculum or after school club. However, before investing the required funds, they will want to know precisely how you intend to use robots in your classroom to assist your learners with mastering academic standards, getting career-ready, and possibly preparing students for competitive robotics.

Therefore, be ready to discuss how robotics will help meet some of the performance expectations for students as dictated by your local academic standards and school district. Content and elective teachers should also understand the correlations to the ISTE and CSTA standards and be able to explain this to your administrators.

2. Create a written plan of how robotics will meet the academic needs of students.

I suggest that your written plan include a lesson plan(s) and a one-pager explaining how robotics will help students meet some of the performance expectations as dictated by your local academic standards and school district. I would be very specific about the performance tasks that are the follow-through of learning goals in your standards. Your written plan should also highlight correlations to the ISTE and CSTA standards as a selling point in school districts where either or both of the standards are adopted or adapted.

3. Poll students to gauge their buy-in.

Students must be the number one stakeholder when it comes to the learning—especially when there will be a substantial investment of both time and money, as is the case with robotics. It is important to note that obtaining student support for robotics in the classroom will only require their commitment to both safety and learning. However, if you are seeking to start an after-school club, you will need both their and their parents' commitment to staying after school and perhaps attending competitive events on some weekends. For an afterschool club, you will most likely need a solid list of committed students before getting your administration to sign off.

4. Create a list of needed items and a budget.

This is a critical part of the approval process. The key here is to determine a dollar amount early on. Prices for robotics tools will vary and will need to be determined by your goals of how they will be used. For example, if you plan to use robotics in the classroom, you should focus less on robots that require an elaborate build and more on robots you can program. To help eliminate the guesswork for educators reading this book, recommendations for each of the content areas are provided in part two, along with enough curriculum to get you started. Teachers wishing to start an afterschool club for competitive robotics can read the final chapter of this book for tips and should also contact local community groups that organize robotics events for the appropriate budget and other pertinent guidelines. For long-distance competitive events, include a travel budget accounting for expenses such as hotels, transportation, and food.

5. Create a realistic timeline.

This part is critical for meeting deadlines and keeping track of all that needs to be done on this list. If you are new to this process and unsure of how long certain items take to accomplish, use guesstimates and seek the advice of a colleague who has already accomplished what you are trying to accomplish. Also, elicit helpers for meeting some of the action items on your timeline.

6. Find teacher and parent helpers.

If you are starting an afterschool club to pursue competitive robotics, it is imperative to elicit the assistance of a colleague or two as well as a few parents. I encourage you to seek out folks that already have a passion for robotics, some experience, or a sincere interest to work with kids in this capacity. They will be extremely helpful to you in tasks such as helping students learn to build and program the robots, transporting equipment, supervising groups of students, bringing snacks, and providing moral support.

7. Determine storage and meeting location.

Classroom robots are typically easier to store than competitive robots because they require less space. So, if your tools require considerable space and your classroom closet won't do the trick, it is important to determine a location that will be fully accessible as needed. Communication is the key here, especially if the designated storage and meeting areas are in another teacher's space. Be sure to keep everyone in the loop regarding when you will need access. Creating and posting a meeting schedule can be helpful and is recommended for this purpose.

Another item to remember is that your meeting area will need to accommodate students working on their robot builds, programming, and testing their designs in action. I like to create a space with a field that is a replica of the competition field that students will be competing on because it allows them to practice for the real thing.

8. Keep communication open.

Whether you are using educational robotics in the classroom or after school, it is important to check in and have frequent communication with all of your stakeholders (including school administration, district leaders, industry partners, and parents). I recommend meeting face-to-face quarterly (once every nine weeks of the school year) and keeping stakeholders informed through either email or a monthly newsletter.

9. Use social media.

If you are not using Twitter, Instagram, or other social media tools to promote your students' work, you should consider getting connected! Create a handle that captures the essence of your classroom or afterschool club. Create or use a district hashtag. Be sure to tag your stakeholders and share examples of your students in action. Remember to obtain permission from both your school administration and parents/guardians before posting images of your students.

10. Improve your own learning gaps.

If you are not yet proficient with the robotics tools you plan to introduce to students; it will be important for you to develop enough expertise to facilitate the learning. This doesn't require a lengthy learning curve, but it does require consistency—and 30 to 40 minutes a day will suffice. See the next section for tips on connecting with other colleagues through a professional learning network (PLN) for this purpose.

Do Not Go at the Learning Alone—Join a PLN!

If you are new to the field and want to learn how to leverage robotics and other edtech for augmenting instruction and also find likeminded educators, consider joining a professional learning network.

Think of a PLN as a support system and a familiar place where you and colleagues can go to learn and share. Having this type of support system can make leveling up your use of edtech and planning for instruction around it less daunting.

ISTE currently supports 22 PLNs. These are highly effective for assisting educators with both knowledge acquisition and practice enhancement by participating in collaborative professional development, the study of pedagogical approaches, and best practices in our profession. I belong to both the Computer Science and STEM PLNs to collaborate with colleagues and enhance my professional learning.

You can also form or join a PLN at your school or organization, preferably within your grade level team, because it will be strategic support for helping teachers who all teach the same students. Allying with colleagues outside of your grade level is also useful when vertically aligning the learning experiences of students, which makes it easier to correlate your instruction with both CS and ISTE standards.

 RESOURCE

Improving Teaching and Learning with Edtech

Edutopia–*Leveling up your use of edtech* (edut.to/301VjKE) This how-to-blog shares advice

 on learning to use and teach new edtech.

Access to Edtech, Advocacy, Grants, and Equity

Once you have your team assembled (or even if you're flying solo), all efforts should focus on securing what's not available to students but is critical to their immediate educational needs—such as curriculum, professional development, and edtech.

RESOURCE

Become an Edtech Advocate!

ISTE: *Edtech advocate in 3 easy steps* (bit.ly/2C4MipD) How-to blog for becoming an edtech advocate and

 leveraging your ISTE affiliate.

Some of the most common roadblocks—for example, lack of edtech accessibility and funding or not knowing how to use a new robotics tool—are typically amplified by "not knowing what we do not know." This should not deter or frustrate us. If the needed edtech or robotics tools are already in your building or school district, make a written request for their use. Always have a rationale for how the tool will meet the academic needs of your students (this could be included in a lesson plan) and include that in your request. If you do not have a plan yet and are looking to create one, only request one device and specify that you will use it to tinker, learn, plan, and explore how it could be used to enhance instruction. Typically, these types of requests are not denied.

If there is no access to the robotics tool (or edtech) you want, understand that this is an equity issue and you will need to either advocate for access or apply for a grant. Regardless of the method you choose, you will still require a plan for how the tool will meet the academic needs of students (see step number two in the previous section). Most school systems have offices of educational technology, career and technical education (CTE), and Title 1. These programs are federally funded and already have budget lines allocated for edtech tools including, but not limited to, robotics.

Grants

Many schools have access to academic enrichment grants (i.e., Title II and IV block grant funding) that can provide you with the right tools and training (DoED, 2016). With your plan in hand, start making your case there. You will most likely find that someone in your district is already involved with or doing robotics and this could be an opportunity to collaborate and strengthen your PLN.

Most school systems also have grant departments whose job is to stay informed about the latest and most popular grant opportunities available nationally or in your state or region. Before contacting them, it is best to get the blessing of your building administrator(s) and just as in the previous scenarios, be prepared with your plan!

When dealing with grant departments and writers, it is always best to have your plan for the use of robotics and associated edtech in typed format. For ideas for your written plan, please see step number two at the beginning of this chapter. Once you have settled on a specific grant, always request to see the questions/stipulations of the grant and provide as much information to the writers as possible. This can speed up the process of having a timely and completed submission.

Some good grants for robotics to consider include the following:

- **National Endowment for the Arts (NEA) Grants (arts.gov/grants)**

- **National Science Foundation (NSF) Grants (nsf.gov/funding)**

- **Northrop Grumman Robotics Grants (bit.ly/2msGUrN)**

- **Pearson STEM Grants (pearsonschool.com/index.cfm?locator=PSZuE4)**

- **PITSCO Education Grants (pitsco.com/Experience-Pitsco/Grants-and-Funding)**

- **Rural Technology Fund (ruraltechfund.org)**

- **The Spencer Foundation (spencer.org)**

Robotics and Educational Equity

This chapter focuses on providing educators the needed know-how in preparing for robotics in terms of obtaining school buy-in, edtech, and effective teacher preparation. Because we have already established in chapter one that learning educational robotics provides students with real-world learning relevant to today's careers, it is important to dedicate a portion of this chapter to teacher preparation as a major component of how learning with robotics truly becomes a part of an equitable education. This is critical as it enables robotics or CS classes to be effective and not simply a visible component in our school buildings.

RESOURCE

Focusing on Equity in CS Education

ISTE: *Focus on equity to ensure that all students are 'CS' material* (bit.ly/2TIWaeC) How-to blog for using best

 practices for equity in CS.

According to the Center for Public Education (2016), educational equity is *only* achieved when *all* students receive the resources they need to graduate successfully.

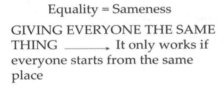

Equality = Sameness

GIVING EVERYONE THE SAME
THING ———→ It only works if
everyone starts from the same
place

Equity = Fairness

ACCESS TO THE SAME
OPPORTUNITIES ———→ We
must first ensure equity before we
can enjoy equality

Figure 2.1: Equality vs. Equity. Source: Elmina B. Sewall
Foundation. Artist: Saskatoon Health Region.

Therefore, the right way to think about robotics and CS in our education system
is that it is foundational. Part of that foundation also means that we need to develop
highly qualified teachers if our students are going to be fully prepared when they
leave the K–12 system. Excellent teachers need to be included in the resources students need to graduate successfully. I believe this helps level the playing field for students furthest from opportunity and is a major step in achieving the fairness depicted
in Figure 2.1 by the Elmina B. Sewall Foundation. I like to think of our teachers (met-
aphorically) as part of the materials needed to strengthen the crates in the image. For
appropriate assembly, crates require the right wood, hand and power tools, screws or
nails, measurement, and symmetry for sturdiness. When our teachers are well versed
and know how to teach the material correctly, they provide a portion of that sturdiness to the crates by bringing to life the curriculum and incorporating edtech tools.

Keeping educational equity and deeper learning in mind as the ultimate outcome
for all students engaged in learning about robotics, this book is designed for
teachers to use as a guide for helping them apply the necessary rigor levels deemed
appropriate and in context with their content area (ELA, mathematics, science, and
social studies) and at all stages of instruction.

Teaching Foundational Knowledge and Skills for Robotics

Having an idea of where we want our students to take the intended learning in our robotics lessons is critical. We need to begin with the end in mind, by identifying both the knowledge and skills we want them to acquire—not just for our lessons but for life. This practice is beneficial for assisting educators with guiding planning and reframing content standards and big ideas.

I often assist educators with backward design planning. We categorize both knowledge and skills into the following five categories:

1. Content Knowledge

2. Technology Skills

3. Workplace Skills

4. Community Engagement and Civic Responsibility

5. Career Exploration

These categories are derived from the "profile of a Virginia graduate" (VDOE, 2016) and many departments of education now use something similar.

For designing rich interdisciplinary lessons and projects for teaching robotics effectively, these are some of the key items that are critical for each of the categories:

- **Content Knowledge:** ELA (reading and writing), math (algorithms), science (energy, forces, and motion), computational thinking, engineering, and coding/programming

- **Technology Skills:** Working knowledge of motors, gears, sensors, microcontrollers, apps, the internet, and relevant devices

- **Workplace Skills:** Technology savviness, collaboration with others, empathy, punctuality, people skills, and soft skills

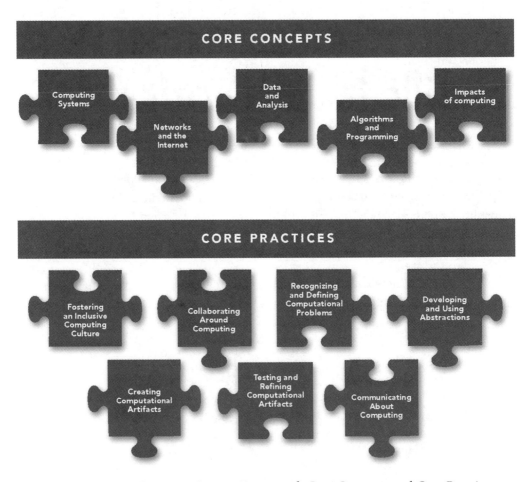

Figure 3.1: K–12 Computer Science Framework Core Concepts and Core Practices.

- **Community Engagement and Civic Responsibility:** Volunteer, global citizen, advocate

- **Career Exploration:** Learning about relevant careers, meeting professionals, and creating a career pathway. Older students can participate in internships, job shadowing, or work-based learning.

RESOURCE

Resources for Developing Technologically Literate Graduates

ISTE: *Portrait of technologically literate graduate* (bit.ly/2UZbfKm)

How-to blog for developing technologically literate students.

Once the intended outcomes are identified, it is important for educators to understand that students must learn and transfer the items while creating products and working on several projects. One lesson or experience will not help them become great computer scientists or engineers or learn all there is to know about coding, programming, and building circuits in the context of robotics. They must design and create multiple products that infuse the CS core concepts and practices found in the K-12 Computer Science Framework (see Figure 3.1) throughout their K–8 experience. Educators should familiarize themselves with the framework, core concepts, and practices.

Learning Robotics Is a Journey, Not a Mad Dash

Teaching robotics can appear daunting, but it doesn't have to be when we teach our kids how to think critically, problem solve, and follow logical steps. When working with students, our goal should always be fostering their deeper learning and building their capacity for more rigorous tasks, which they cannot accomplish if we skip critical components of knowledge to get through instruction.

In my previous position with Richmond Public Schools, our teachers were also new to robotics so they learned alongside their students. As a result, we fine tuned our teaching approach by facilitating teaching and learning experiences following these four steps:

1. Beginning with computational thinking (CT)

2. Designing/building robots

3. Programming

4. Coding

We found learning robotics in this particular order to be the right scaffold needed for providing both teachers and students the foundational understanding and skills required for further study and more complex tasks. Moreover, those who developed the interest could expand their skills by joining a robotics team or afterschool club, and those who did not now had the awareness.

Know Your Options and How to Begin

In grades 1-8, getting students started in robotics is relatively easy when we know how to choose the right tools and understand our options. In my previous role as a curriculum specialist, our afterschool clubs used both the LEGO Mindstorms robot and the *VEX* IQ Kit as the intro and the VEX EDR robot for high schoolers. We chose these two options because the Richmond Virginia area (RVA) hosts both FIRST Robotics (with grades 1-12 using LEGO) and RVA Robotics (with grades 1-12 using VEX) competitions. Many of the parents in our school system wanted this option for their children, and we accommodated them with including robotics in the curriculum, in afterschool clubs, and by forming teams for competitive events.

If you are faced with similar options, decide if you wish to engage your students in competitive events before purchasing your robots. Understand that if you do compete, there are considerable costs in both time and money that will need to be budgeted for. Then make an informed decision after discovering which events are popular and easily accessible in your area. It is essential to get the support of both parents and district building leaders if you choose to go this route.

When teaching robotics in the classroom (not after school), robots that require less elaborate builds come in more cost-effective options for all grade levels. Some of these options include Sphero, Ozobot, littleBits, and others. These will not require participation in competitive events or a lot of cleanup. The main focus would be the intended learning of your students.

These are the four steps you can take to help your students understand key concepts and programming regardless of your robot or platform:

1. **Build the robot (when applicable):** This is a great entry point for students new to robotics and many younger kids will love this step.

2. **Learn the basics:** Through exploring tutorials and playing, students will need to learn about motors, sensors, gears, and other components associated with the edtech you choose.

3. **Learn to program:** Most devices will have built-in missions, which enable students to see how to make the robot move with motors and respond to touch or motion with sensors. As they became more accustomed to the built-in programs, they can start making their own programs using visual programming blocks (such as ROBOLAB and others).

4. **Make curricular connections to CS, STEM, and content areas:** This step helps significantly to elucidate the concepts of computational thinking into practice. Connections to the content areas will be fully elaborated on in part two of this book.

In the upcoming chapters we will unpack these four steps further and with specific lessons. However, it is important to put first things first so that our learning is logical for building our capacity and understanding.

RESOURCE

Knowing the Top Two Organizations That Make Robotics for Education

LEGO Education
(lego.build/2FBkidV)

LEGO education solutions for various grade levels.

VEX Robotics (bit.ly/2ODRdTu)
Tools to inspire and guide

problem solving at various grade levels.

Robotics and Computational Thinking

U nless you've been hiding under a rock or perhaps just too busy to be paying attention, you'll know about the current trend in K–12 education to have schools incorporate computational thinking into classroom instruction. However, CT isn't new. Let's briefly explore its historical uses, gain a better understanding of how it's applied, and get some additional resources for CT before integrating it with robotics.

Computer scientist Seymour Papert was the first to use the term CT in education (1980) and advocated for a pragmatic approach to knowledge construction using computers and the Logo educational programming language. Papert believed this could assist learners in developing powerful critical thinking and reasoning skills. Shortly after that, theoretical physicist Ken Wilson made significant advances in the field of computational science with computer software that used detailed algorithms to carry out simulations. Consequently, leaders in computational science used CT to describe the habits of mind they developed, and many reported learning CT by designing computations, instead of studying CS (Guzdial, 2015).

In 2006, CT was introduced in education by CS professor Jeannette Wing (Wing 2006). She described CT as a thinking tool used to solve problems and promoted the idea that CT builds on both human and computing processes. The field of computing education research became revitalized due to Wing's introduction, along with well-publicized breakthroughs in computational science and rapid digitization of society's infrastructure and industry's major functions.

Then, with the support of scientists who applied CT across various fields as well as congress, CS was included in the definition of STEM in 2015, and the National Science Foundation (NSF) supported the current movement to incorporate both CT and CS into K–12 education.

Table 4.1 Introducing the four elements of CT to students

CT ELEMENT	DESCRIPTION	METHOD FOR INTRODUCING
Decomposition	Decomposition helps learners break down complex problems into easier to manage pieces.	The best way to start is with a task they already do. Like brushing their teeth, tying a shoelace, or making breakfast.
Pattern Recognition	Pattern recognition is mapping similarities and differences in decomposed problems, which is an important skill to have for making predictions.	This can be introduced to students by showing them images of various animals, desserts, or even text.
Abstraction	Abstraction is simply the process of taking away or removing features from something in order to make a set of essential features. It has also been described as the process of removing unnecessary features or removing the fluff (which I like).	The abstraction process can be leveraged by having students plan a party, vacation, or trip to the movies and then solve problems by removing all irrelevant details and patterns.
Algorithm design	Algorithm design is creating step-by-step logical series of instructions (algorithms) for solving problems.	Start students out by having them create logical steps to completing a familiar task and then have them flowchart it using the recommended universal symbols.

Although there is no exact definition of CT, it is widely accepted in education that CT has four elements (decomposition, abstraction, pattern recognition, and algorithm design) and that learning and applying CT helps learners understand the logic and algorithmic processes that are the foundation of both hardware and software designs. I, therefore, believe that using CT is critical for designing and working with robotics. Furthermore, educators can leverage the power of CT as a higher-order problem-solving skill by helping students build competency in CT by developing their versatility for recognizing and applying the four elements of CT to everyday situations before doing so with robotics. Table 4.1 shares a breakdown of the four elements along with suggested methods for introducing them to students.

How CT Differs from CS

Simply put, computational thinking is a problem-solving process (or set of processes and skills). Computer science (CS) is a discipline, CT is not.

RESOURCE

Resources for Computational Thinking

ISTE: *Computational thinking for all* (bit.ly/30cDqsV)

How-to blog with a plethora of CT resources.

ISTE: *How to develop computational thinkers* (bit.ly/2HONOjU)
How-to blog with strategies for developing computational thinkers across the disciplines.

According to the K–12 Computer Science Framework (2016), CS is a discipline that is part of computing education. Computing education in K–12 schools includes computer literacy, educational technology, digital citizenship, information technology, and computer science (p. 13). As the foundation for all computing, computer science is "the study of computers and algorithmic processes, including their principles, their hardware and software designs, their applications, and their impact on society" (Tucker et. al, 2006, p. 2).

Because CT is a problem-solving skill, it can also be applied in disciplines other than computer science. This book aims to eliminate a lot of the guesswork for educators from the various disciplines attempting to implement CT by providing a plethora of ready-to-use resources in the forthcoming pages.

The K–12 Computer Science Framework is an excellent source for either beginning or improving our understanding of how to incorporate CT into instruction. The framework focuses on core concepts and core practices that describe what students should know about CT/

Core Practices
+ Computational Thinking

Practices 1, 2, and 7:
General practices
of CS that support
computational
thinking

Practices 3–6:
Computational
thinking practices

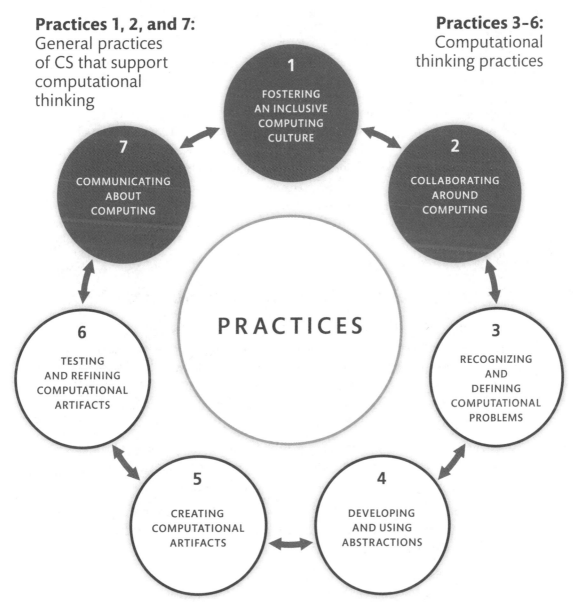

Figure 4.1: K–12 Computer Science Framework Core Practices
Highlighting Computational Thinking.

CS and what they should be able to do with that knowledge. It also shows how to connect CT/CS to other learning (i.e., ELA, math, science, engineering, etc.). The diagram of the core practices (shown in Figure 4.1) shows as shaded circles those practices (1, 2, and 7) that support CT.

To complement both the K–12 Computer Science Framework and the CSTA K–12 Computer Science Standards for Students, ISTE developed the CT Competencies for educators to help schools integrate CT across all disciplines and with all students by correlating it to what they already teach.

It is also important for teachers to understand that the CS standards and CT Competencies are not just about programming and coding; and were intentionally written to align with the academic subjects that they teach. Now that computers are part of everything we do and educational technology must be used by all teachers to augment instruction, these competencies are extremely helpful with assisting learners with becoming computational thinkers who can leverage computing to solve problems innovatively.

ISTE Computational Thinking Competencies

▶ 1. Computational Thinking (Learner)

Educators continually improve their practice by developing an understanding of computational thinking and its application as a cross-curricular skill. Educators develop a working knowledge of core components of computational thinking: such as decomposition; gathering and analyzing data; abstraction; algorithm design; and how computing impacts people and society. Educators:

    a. Set professional learning goals to explore and apply teaching strategies for integrating CT practices into learning activities in ways that enhance student learning of both the academic discipline and CS concepts.

    b. Learn to recognize where and how computation can be used to enrich data or content to solve discipline-specific problems and be able to connect these opportunities to foundational CT practices and CS concepts.

    c. Leverage CT and CS experts, resources and professional learning networks to continuously improve practice integrating CT across content areas.

    d. Develop resilience and perseverance when approaching CS and CT learning experiences, build comfort with ambiguity and open-ended problems, and see failure as an opportunity to learn and innovate.

    e. Recognize how computing and society interact to create opportunities, inequities, responsibilities and threats for individuals and organizations.

▶ *2. Equity Leader (Leader)*

All students and educators have the ability to be computational thinkers and CS learners. Educators proactively counter stereotypes that exclude students from opportunities to excel in computing and foster an inclusive and diverse classroom culture that incorporates and values unique perspectives; builds student self-efficacy and confidence around computing; addresses varying needs and strengths; and addresses bias in interactions, design and development methods. Educators:

    a. Nurture a confident, competent and positive identity around computing for every student.

    b. Construct and implement culturally relevant learning activities that address a diverse range of ethical, social and cultural perspectives on computing and highlight computing achievements from diverse role models and teams.

    c. Choose teaching approaches that help to foster an inclusive computing culture, avoid stereotype threat and equitably engage all students.

    d. Assess and manage classroom culture to drive equitable student participation, address exclusionary dynamics and counter implicit bias.

    e. Communicate with students, parents and leaders about the impacts of computing in our world and across diverse roles and professional life, and why these skills are essential for all students.

▶ *3. Collaborating Around Computing (Collaborator)*

Effective collaboration around computing requires educators to incorporate diverse perspectives and unique skills when developing student learning opportunities, and recognize that collaboration skills must be explicitly taught in order to lead to better outcomes than individuals working independently. Educators work together to select tools and design activities and environments that facilitate these collaborations and outcomes. Educators:

    a. Model and learn with students how to formulate computational solutions to problems and how to give and receive actionable feedback.

b. Apply effective teaching strategies to support student collaboration around computing, including pair programming, working in varying team roles, equitable workload distribution and project management.

c. Plan collaboratively with other educators to create learning activities that cross disciplines to strengthen student understanding of CT and CS concepts and transfer application of knowledge in new contexts.

▶ 4. Creativity & Design (Designer)

Computational thinking skills can empower students to create computational artifacts that allow for personal expression. Educators recognize that design and creativity can encourage a growth mindset and work to create meaningful CS learning experiences and environments that inspire students to build their skills and confidence around computing in ways that reflect their interests and experiences. Educators:

a. Design CT activities where data can be obtained, analyzed and represented to support problem-solving and learning in other content areas.

b. Design authentic learning activities that ask students to leverage a design process to solve problems with awareness of technical and human constraints and defend their design choices.

c. Guide students on the importance of diverse perspectives and human-centered design in developing computational artifacts with broad accessibility and usability.

d. Create CS and CT learning environments that value and encourage varied viewpoints, student agency, creativity, engagement, joy and fun.

▶ 5. Integrating Computational Thinking (Facilitator)

Educators facilitate learning by integrating computational thinking practices into the classroom. Since computational thinking is a foundational skill, educators develop every student's ability to recognize opportunities to apply computational thinking in their environment. Educators:

a. Evaluate and use CS and CT curricula, resources and tools that account for learner variability to meet the needs of all students.

b. Empower students to select personally meaningful computational projects.

c. Use a variety of instructional approaches to help students frame problems in ways that can be represented as computational steps or algorithms to be performed by a computer.

d. Establish criteria for evaluating CT practices and content learning that use a variety of formative and alternative assessments to enable students to demonstrate their understanding of age-appropriate CS and CT vocabulary, practices and concepts.

As you can see, there is a lot to unpack within the indicators of the CT competencies. In the context of robotics, my suggestion is to focus on how you want to teach CT and see evidence of its elements as students plan, build robots, program robots, and test and evaluate their designs and final solutions. Also, bear in mind that these competencies serve as guidelines for you to unpack and correlate to the standards in your content area—in tandem with the many of the concepts and practices found in the K–12 Computer Science Framework and the CSTA K–12 Computer Science Standards for Students.

Introduction to Computational Thinking for Every Educator (ISTE U Course)

To assist educators with building and exploring digital age competencies (spanning hot topics in both computer science and edtech), ISTE has created ISTE U.

ISTE U is a curation of engaging professional learning experiences via a virtual hub for educators to experience anywhere and at their own pace. The courses are eligible for graduate-level credit through the Continuing Education and Professional Development Department at Dominican University of California.

The Introduction to Computational Thinking for Every Educator course was developed in collaboration with Google to guide and supports educators as they design and plan lessons that integrate CT across all disciplines and grade levels. Moreover, the course increases both awareness and understanding of how CT can be incorporated into a school's curricula plan.

RESOURCE

Integrate CT with the ISTE CT Competencies

ISTE Computational Thinking Competencies for Educators (bit.ly/2CVPdBt)

Integrate CT across disciplines and with all students.

RESOURCE

Get support for CT integration with ISTE U!

ISTE U: *Introduction to Computational Thinking for Every Educator* (bit.ly/2V91MGA) Online course assisting educators with integrating computational

thinking across all disciplines and grade levels.

Start Teaching Computational Thinking with Unplugged Lessons

The purpose of beginning CT with unplugged activities is to help students make connections between CT and previous learning, to clear up any misconceptions about CT, and to promote critical thinking and problem-solving in fun and engaging ways while building the right background knowledge needed for CS skills such as designing and programming robots. The lessons are labeled unplugged because they are taught without using computers or tech tools.

So, if you're wanting to engage students who are new to CT and CS and do not have any prior knowledge, look no further than CS Unplugged (csunplugged.org) for a variety of unplugged activities. Some of which include the following:

1. **Binary numbers:** Six lessons, ages 5-10 with connections to art, literacy, and Music.

2. **Kidbots:** Four lessons, ages 5-10 with four curriculum integrations and 50 programming challenges.

3. **Sorting networks:** Four lessons, ages 5-14 with four curriculum integrations.

4. **Error detection and correction:** Three lessons, ages 5-10 with five curriculum integrations and 24 programming challenges.

5. **Searching algorithms:** Six lessons, ages 5-10 with four curriculum integrations.

 RESOURCE

CS Unplugged Lessons and Printables

CS Unplugged: *Unplugged computer science lessons*

 (csunplugged.org) Teach computer science without a computer!

Unplugged Lesson

Computational Thinking

The following Code.org unplugged lesson is one that I highly recommend teachers use when starting to teach CT. The lesson doesn't have a specific grade level and can be adapted to most K–8 scenarios and content areas. However, K–2 teachers will need to provide more scaffolds to support students who are not yet able to read.

 Unplugged Lesson: Computational Thinking
code.org/curriculum/course3/1/Teacher

Overview

In this lesson, students build competence for the four CT elements (decomposition, pattern matching, abstraction, and algorithms) by using examples of what fictional players have done to figure out how to play an actual game. As students learn to put into practice the four elements of CT in one cohesive activity, the lesson provides them with the foundational problem-solving skills needed for designing and programming with robotics. Think of it as stacking building blocks to form the foundation for a much bigger and more complex structure.

The lesson provides steps for teachers to take for the following:

- Unpacking the vocabulary for CT

- Reinforcing the CT practices for students with user experience scripts found in the CT kit

- Pattern matching and abstraction with a color, animals, and an object

- Pattern matching is augmented mathematically when adding and finally multiplying. Here teachers can help students follow the same steps but with different numbers as the lesson suggests, ensuring they understand the concepts but in different scenarios

- CT assessment

Duration

The basic lesson time is 25 minutes and only includes the activity. If time permits, introductory and wrap-up suggestions can be implemented to dive deeper into the subject matter, extend work time, and allow you to make concrete connections to robotics and programming. It is also important to note that time will vary depending on your students' reading and writing ability. My suggestion is to build in some flex time and allow for multiple opportunities to display mastery.

Objectives

STUDENTS WILL

- Analyze information to draw conclusions
- Match identical portions of similar phrases to match patterns
- Identify differences in similar phrases and abstract them out

Vocabulary

The lesson introduces students to the 4 elements of CT.

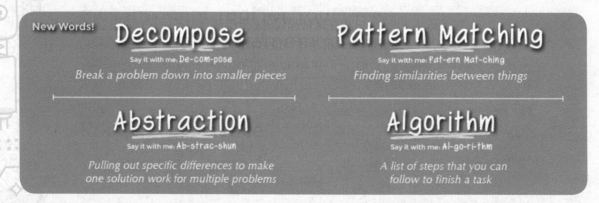

Figure 4.2: Computational thinking lesson vocabulary.

Students who are not independent readers yet will need assistance with sounding out the elements. Tips on sounding out each of the elements by syllable are provided along with the definitions (see Figure 4.2).

Materials, Resources, and Teacher Prep

FOR STUDENTS

- One die per group

- One Computational Thinking Kit per group

- Pens, pencils, and scissors

- Computational Thinking Assessment for each student

FOR TEACHER

- Lesson video

- Teacher lesson guide

- One printed Computational Thinking Kit for each group

- One printed Computational Thinking Assessment for each student

Warm Up

Inform students that they will sum up all the numbers between 1 and 200.

- To ease any anxieties that they may have, be sure to express that this is not a graded exercise.

- Now, inform them that they must do it all in their heads.

- Add the time constraint of thirty seconds.

- They may feel overwhelmed. This is intentional. You can indicate with your tone and demeanor that you might be crazy asking this of them but begin timing with a resounding: "Starting NOW."

- Watch the class as you keep time. How many are lost in thought?

When time is up, ask if anyone was able to get the total.

- Ask if there is anyone who thought the problem was so hard that they didn't even attempt it.

- Did anyone attempt it and just not finish? What did they try?

- Guide students toward thinking a little smaller.

Explain, "If we break the problem up into smaller pieces, it becomes easier to manage."

- Let's start at the two ends. What is 200 + 1?

- What is 199 + 2?

- What is 198 + 3?

- See a pattern?

Ask, "How many of these pairs will we have?"

- What is the last pair we will find? 100 + 101.

- That means that we have 100 total pairs.

- If we have 100 total pairs of sums of 201, how do we find the final total?

- What is 100 × 201?

Ask, "Now, what if we wanted to find the trick to do this with other numbers?"

- Can we do it easily with 2,000?

- How about 20,000?

- What stays the same? What is different?

- If we use abstractions to make our end goal something that can change (say we name it "blank") then we can make an algorithm that will work for any number.

- Work through the problem until you ultimately arrive at

$$? = (\text{"blank"}/2) \times (\text{"blank"}+1)$$

- Do a few simple examples to show that the algorithm is correct for

$$\text{blanks} = 2, 3, 4, \text{ and } 5$$

Finally, you can say something like this: "This is all to show that if you use the tools of computational thinking (decomposition, pattern matching, abstraction, and algorithms), you can figure out how to solve problems that no one has already taught you how to solve . . . just like we did here! This will be an extremely powerful skill for the rest of your life!"

Activities (25 min)

Computational Thinking

This lesson is all about a "Game with No Instructions." Students will be charged with figuring out how to play the game as a small group. The small details of their final algorithm are unimportant. What *is* important is that they were able to take a huge task like figuring out how to play a game on their own and take small steps toward achieving the goal.

Students will be guided toward discovering the rules using the steps of computational thinking. Resist the temptation to point the students toward "doing it right" and instead allow them to just do it on their own. If they feel stumped or confused, encourage the students to look at the information that has been given to them, or if they must, allow them to ask a classmate.

Directions

1. Divide students into groups of 2–4.

2. Have the groups read over user experiences to get an idea of how other students have played the "Game with No Instructions."

3. Encourage them to pattern match between each experience by circling the sections of words that are identical from player to player.

4. Next, have them abstract away differences from each experience by underlining words that change from player to player.

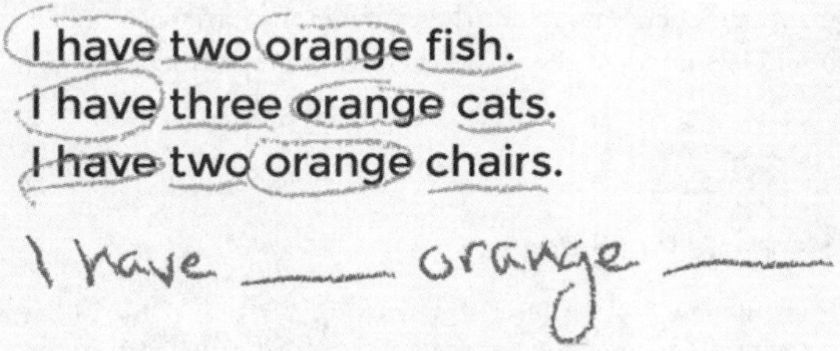

I have two orange fish.
I have three orange cats.
I have two orange chairs.

I have ___ orange ___

Figure 4.3: Finding patterns in computational
thinking unplugged lesson.

5. Using pattern matching and abstraction, have them make a script template for gameplay by writing up the circled parts of the other students' experiences and leaving the underlined sections as blanks (see Figure 4.3).

6. Give students a blank sheet of paper to write a list of instructions for how they think this game should be played based on the user experiences that they just read. This will be their algorithm.

7. Have students play the game using the algorithm that they just made. Each player should get at least two turns.

Reflection and Wrap-Up (5 min)

What did we learn? Intended to get students thinking about the big picture and how the lesson relates to real-world situations, these questions can be discussed as a class, in groups, or among partners.

- What should you try to do when you're asked to do something and you don't know how?

- If a problem is too hard, what should you try to do?

- If you find similarities in lots of solutions to different problems, what does that probably tell you?

- If you have a problem that is just a little different from a problem that you have a solution for, what would you do?

Assessment (10 min)

- Hand out the assessment worksheet and allow students to complete the activity independently after the instructions have been well explained. This should feel familiar, thanks to the previous activities.

Standards Addressed

ISTE Standards for Students

- **1.a.** Articulate and set personal learning goals, develop strategies leveraging technology to achieve them and reflect on the learning process itself to improve learning outcomes.

- **3.d.** Build knowledge by actively exploring real-world issues and problems, developing ideas and theories and pursuing answers and solutions.

- **4.a.** Build knowledge by actively exploring real-world issues and problems, developing ideas and theories and pursuing answers and solutions.

- **5.a.** Formulate problem definitions suited for technology-assisted methods such as data analysis, abstract models and algorithmic thinking in exploring and finding solutions.

- **5.c.** Break problems into component parts, extract key information, and develop descriptive models to understand complex systems or facilitate problem-solving.

CSTA K-12 Computer Science Standards

- **CPP.L1:6-05.** Construct a program as a set of step-by-step instructions to be acted out.

- **CT.L1:6-02.** Develop a simple understanding of an algorithm using computer-free exercises.

- **CT.L2-01.** Use the basic steps in algorithmic problem solving to design solutions.

- **CT.L2-06.** Describe and analyze a sequence of instructions being followed.

- **CT.L2-08.** Use visual representations of problem states, structures, and data.

- **CT.L2-12.** Use abstraction to decompose a problem into sub problems.

- **CT.L2-14.** Examine connections between elements of mathematics and computer science including binary numbers, logic, sets, and functions.

NGSS Science and Engineering Practices

- **3-5-ETS1-2.** Generate and compare multiple possible solutions to a problem based on how well each is likely to meet the criteria and constraints of the problem.

Common Core Mathematical Practices

- Make sense of problems and persevere in solving them.

- Reason abstractly and quantitatively.

- Construct viable arguments and critique the reasoning of others.

- Attend to precision.

- Look for and make use of structure.

- Look for and express regularity in repeated reasoning.

Common Core Math Standards

- **3.OA.3.** Use multiplication and division within 100 to solve word problems in situations involving equal groups, arrays, and measurement quantities.

- **4.NBT.B.4.** Fluently add and subtract multi-digit whole numbers using the standard algorithm.

- **5.NBT.B.5.** Fluently multiply multi-digit whole numbers using the standard algorithm.

Common Core Language Arts Standards

- **SL.3.1.** Engage effectively in a range of collaborative discussions (one-on-one, in groups, and teacher-led) with diverse partners on grade 3 topics and texts, building on others' ideas and expressing their own clearly.

- **SL.3.3.** Ask and answer questions about information from a speaker, offering appropriate elaboration and detail.

- **L.3.6.** Acquire and use accurately grade-appropriate conversational, general academic, and domain-specific words and phrases, including those that signal spatial and temporal relationships.

- **SL.4.1.** Engage effectively in a range of collaborative discussions (one-on-one, in groups, and teacher-led) with diverse partners on grade 4 topics and texts, building on others' ideas and expressing their own clearly.

- **L.4.6.** Acquire and use accurately grade-appropriate general academic and domain-specific words and phrases, including those that signal precise actions, emotions, or states of being and that are basic to a particular topic.

- **SL.5.1.** Engage effectively in a range of collaborative discussions (one-on-one, in groups, and teacher-led) with diverse partners on grade 5 topics and texts, building on others' ideas and expressing their own clearly.

- **L.5.6.** Acquire and use accurately grade-appropriate general academic and domain-specific words and phrases, including those that signal contrast, addition, and other logical relationships.

CHAPTER 5

Robotics and Programming Demystified in Actionable Steps

Robotics involves building and programming robots. Not all educational robots will need to be built, but in most cases they will need to be programmed. So, whether teachers or coaches are teaching robotics in lessons or preparing students for competitive robotics, this chapter is dedicated to simplifying the complex tasks of building and programming into actionable and easy to follow steps.

Moreover, the computational thinking (CT) elements are applied here and many of the indicators in the CT competencies can be captured in the following steps.

Robotics Demystified in Four Steps

As mentioned above, all educational robots do not have to be built (assembly). Some are ready for programing. Examples of this would be the Sphero Mini and the SPRK+. For classroom teachers concerned with time constraints and clean up, these and similar robots are the way to go. However, whether you are building or not, it is vital to understand both the hardware and software pertaining to the robot you're using with students. If you are not building, you can skip step two.

Although I use a VEX robot in the following example, the following steps can be applied to robots that require both building and programming. If you don't have a VEX robot, no worries! What will change for you is the final design because in this case I am describing the build of a Clawbot. So, for now, just focus on learning the concepts and practices pertaining to each of the following four steps.

Note to VEX users: Although deeper learning with a tool like VEX takes time, any learner can achieve mastery through precise and consistent practice. The following four steps are how I recommend teachers proceed with students.

Step 1: Begin with the end in mind and know your hardware.

No one appreciates being asked to do something their instructor hasn't done. For this reason, it is essential for teachers who are coaching students through their first robot build to arrive in class with their own built working model. This synergizes the classroom by giving students the confidence that the learning is not just for them, and that their teachers are just as invested in the process as they are.

Providing some guiding questions is also helpful for beginning with the end in mind:

- How can we use our VEX Clawbot kit to build and program a robot that runs an autonomous figure eight?

- How can we use our VEX Clawbot kit to build and program a robot that is controlled by a human operator using the VEXnet joystick and VEXnet keys to interface with the microcontroller?

Once students have their learning goals, guide them in unboxing their kit. Don't let students who are new to VEX robotics do this alone or in groups. A VEX robot has many moving parts and involves several complex systems. Someone with prior experience must lead this part.

I highly recommend having students categorize each of the parts (along with an explanation of each) into the following four groups:

- Structure   - Motion   - Electronics   - Tools (or other)

Step 2: Build the robot!

Typically, I do not recommend having students follow a tutorial step-by-step, but, due to the complexity of an initial VEX build, I would in this case. The VEX guide for building the Clawbot is an excellent introduction to the robot build and for learning the uses of most of the parts categorized by students in Step 1.

And although their first build will not be open-ended, using a guiding question (like those in Step 1) will enable students to tap into their creativity and resourcefulness when programming their robot.

Students familiar with electronics or robotics such as littleBits or LEGO Mindstorms may already be familiar with the concepts and functions of motors, sensors, gears, and system development. However, the metal/aluminum structures and configuration of the VEXnet system or the new V5 system will most likely be very new to them. For the others, everything they encounter will be new and perhaps intimidating. Give your learners time to explore and learn through guided practice and gradual release of responsibility.

> **Note:** For teachers wishing to teach robotics in the context of their content area, my recommendation is to understand the steps in this chapter prior to jumping to the chapters associated with your content area in part two (chapters 6–10).

Whenever I encounter learners in my workshop with significant expertise in VEX EDR, I assign them an open-ended robot build and program that must adhere to specific criteria and constraints. That keeps them engaged, allows them to expand on their creativity and prevents them from doing all of the heavy mental lifting in a group that often deprives less experienced learners of the vital toil necessary for more in-depth learning.

Step 3: Learn the functions of gears, motors, sensors, and other components.

From their depiction in movies and cartoons, many kids (and adults) think of droids whenever robots are mentioned. However, it's important for them to understand that most robots are not created for appearance (whether human or machine-like) but more so to carry out repetitive actions, tasks, and jobs that are either too dangerous or impossible for humans to do on their own.

Students will also need to understand that magic doesn't make robots work or move efficiently. Instead it's an amalgamation of systems working in concert—systems that rely on electronic controls (such as sensors and microcontrollers) and programming software for instructions.

Even before programming (Step 4), students should learn that motors, wheels, gears, shafts, and pneumatics (among other accessories) are what enables motion in robot mechanisms. For helping them make some of these connections, offer them a couple of the learning targets (LTs). Here are a two LTs that I composed for the Clawbot build:

- I can hear each motor grind when I move the gears behind the wheels on both sides of my robot.

- I can seat the shafts (axles) all the way into each motor.

You can try the following sample troubleshooting questions whenever students get stuck. Bear in mind that you'll most likely need to help them make visual connections by using your teacher-created model (see Step 1).

- Does moving one wheel move the entire system? Do they drive one another? Are they interconnected?

- Does your axle turn but your wheel doesn't? Are you using the correct inserts in the wheels?

- Are your wheels hopping? Are there inserts in the wheels?

Step 4: Learn to program the robot.

Luckily, VEX Robotics provides preloaded default code on the VEX Cortex Microcontroller. After your students have completed a successful Clawbot build and have successfully paired their joystick to the cortex, allow them to run the default program (Note: they won't be able to see the code). For many students, seeing the robot they built move forward and backward, lift and lower its arm, and open and close the claw will make them feel like superstars! Allow them this moment of celebration and be sure to engage them in reflection. Also advise them that they will need to learn programming skills to make their robots move beyond the default program.

Note to teachers: Although this step could be carried out independently by an experienced and patient builder, I recommend pairing your students for the initial build. Uniting the structural and motion components is not an easy task. By working cooperatively, the students will realize the need for teamwork.

Now it's time to really learn how to program. These are the steps I use to coach my students and simplify the process:

- Create a user account with VEX Robotics.

- Go to the ROBOTC for VEX Robotics 4.x page to explore your options and you'll be pleased to see, that there's a fun and easy-to-use graphical option that will keep your students engaged.

- Download ROBOTC. I would consult your IT department for this step as there are options for either individual or multiuser installs (Note: Mac users will need to need to take a few extra steps).

- After your software is installed correctly, update the firmware on both the Cortex and joystick. Note: Due to the many intricate steps, for these tasks I prefer students use video tutorials rather than following my verbal instructions.

- Learners new to C-based programming should start with downloading sample programs.

- Be sure that your programs match your robot's physical configuration. This step is very important, otherwise your setup for motors and sensors will not be correct.

- To get students grounded in the basics, I tend to start them with five sample programs. I think it's important for them to see how code manipulates basic movements—primarily autonomously and in both arcade and tank modes with the joystick.

- As students develop capacity for understanding how to program their robots, allow them to write their own code commands to assign their robots more complex tasks. They can use a ROBOTC syntax reference guide for assistance with either ROBOTC Graphical, ROBOTC NL, and ROBOTC through the process. Also teach them the value of code reuse for making their work easier.

 For this final step, there are quick links that you can access for helping you achieve each of the bulleted items. You can find them at bit.ly/2IfFha0 or by scanning the QR code.

Programming Demystified in Four Steps

Robots are controlled by programming and educational robotics have preloaded code (programs) that students can use when learning to program. With the preloaded missions, my advice is to help students learn to identify how the lines or blocks of code manipulate the movements of the robot.

Depending on the type of programming, your students will program robots that are autonomous, semi-autonomous, and remote-controlled. So essentially, these are three types of robots that perform different tasks when programmed.

- **Autonomous robots.** Robots that are programmed to be autonomous and function independently. They obey the commands in their program and don't need further input from humans.

- **Semi-autonomous robots.** Semi-autonomous means that a programmed robot can do much independently but will still require instructions from a human user periodically.

- **Remote-controlled.** Remote-controlled robots are programmed to respond to inputs and do not make decisions without being told. These robots respond to controllers or inputs through a keyboard

When teaching students to program robots, I also recommend that you teach them how computer programs in the broader sense are designed and how they work. Various core coding commands are also helpful for students to know as they become more experienced with programming robots. Therefore, the remainder of this chapter will focus on the basics of computer programming.

Note: I love using ROBOTC because it assists students with learning real-world C programming skills that are used by both engineers and computer scientists. I highly recommend using the ROBOTC Natural Language Library on the Carnegie Mellon Robotics Academy website (bit.ly/35uAPfx).

Precise and consistent practice in programming will help students construct cross-curricular knowledge in tandem with both academic and CS concepts and practices. As programming is the process of writing a program from start to finish, students receive exposure in the amalgamation of practices 3–6 found in the K–12 Computer Science Framework (shown in Figure 4.1 in the previous chapter).

So, how can we successfully engage students in programming robotics and beyond? Here's how we can do so in four major steps (shown in Figure 5.1).

Programming

Identify the problem	Find a solution	Code it	Test it

Figure 5.1: Programming in four steps.
Source: Quentin Watt Tutorials.

Step 1: Identify the problem.

When students are new to programming robots (or other edtech), we typically start by teaching them how to program and code using tutorials. Although there's nothing wrong with that, we don't want to keep them there.

Usually the writer of a tutorial has already identified both the problem and the solution of the program. This includes determining whether the robot being programmed is autonomous, semi-autonomous, or remote-controlled. The best way for students to learn is by writing their own problems and solutions and creating their own programs. Otherwise, they will focus more on learning to code specific functions in a particular language, which is generally no different than rote memorization, which should be replaced with the development of working memory.

Identifying (or defining) the problem is the most critical part of the programming process as students will need to develop a concrete plan for what their complete program will do. This process involves identifying both the known inputs (or given data) and what is to be obtained via outputs (the result). Although programming isn't a simple process, consistent and precise practice will over time build student confidence in articulating the details on the kind of input, processing, and output desired for their programs.

Step 2: Find a solution.

To find or plan the solution to the problem identified in Step 1 (i.e., the task a robot will complete), students can either create a flowchart or write pseudocode. Experienced programmers can and will use either of these methods to convey program development to clients. For students with artistic inclination, having them choreograph the movements of the robot both physically and with simple sketches may be helpful in this step.

A flowchart is a step-by-step solution to a problem that uses a pictorial representation of the direction of the program and consists of arrows, boxes, and other symbols that represent actions (i.e., input/output, process, etc.). Pseudocode is similar to English and is used to convey the solution with more accuracy than in plain English—but with less meticulousness than required by a formal programming language.

The solution process enables the programmer to focus on the logical flow of the program without having to adhere to the actual syntax used by the programming language for the project.

Use the Correct Grammar

All languages spoken or written require correct grammar—a set of principles that define parameters for constructing a sentence or multiple successive sentences. Similarly, coding requires coders to be able to understand and implement fundamental coding concepts using the appropriate syntax (grammar). This is a requirement no matter the programming language and is very useful for students to understand when programming robots.

Some of the critical concepts that are applied to computer programs through coding include:

- **Inputs:** Users must be able to send information into programs they are interacting with. This can be done with various input devices or feeds. The most common are text files, striking keys on a keyboard, or a data feed from a game controller with a motion sensor. In the context of robotics, inputs are code that pass signals to a controller to enable appropriate behavior, which may include estimating and monitoring a robot's environment. In the example using the VEX EDR robot at the beginning of this chapter, the V5 Robot Brain is the controller which allows for both autonomous and driver control.

- **Outputs:** Once data is inputted into a program, it will need to output responses. Responses are typically outputted to a screen via text or graphics, data to other applications, or sound to a device. Printed documents are also output. In the context of robotics, control outputs manipulate mobility of robots.

Step 3: Code it!

Coding is often confused with programming, but coding is just one part of the programming process. Good coders can create instructions from the solutions (discussed in Step 2) and write them into code for the computer to understand. This is where the algorithmic design skills from computational thinking come into play.

It helps when you think of your problem as a math problem, not because you're always doing a lot of math while programming, but because the thought process is the same. In mathematics we often use algorithmic sets of instructions that we

- **Loops:** A programming structure used in programs to repeat a sequence of instructions until a specific condition is met. The two types of loops students should know how to use are *counting loops* and *conditional loops* (also known as while loop and for loop). In the context of robotics, the while loop can be used to repeat a specific block of code until a condition is met.

- **Functions:** Refers to a section of a program that performs a particular task, and in this context, a function represents a procedure or routine that contains instructions used for output from its input. In the context of robotics, (example from RobotC for VEX) functions are first created and then run independently. Functions are declared using the word "void" and are followed by the name the coder wants to give it (i.e., rotateArm).

- **Conditional Statements (logic):** The ability to apply this concept makes programming powerful—as it enables the capability in applications to test a variable against a value and act in a specific way if the condition is met by it (the variable) or differently if it is not. An example of this can be a logic statement for an operation that is evaluated to be either true or false. If and if/else statements are also an example of conditional statements and are the most common syntax across programming languages. Moreover, if/else statements are commonly used to help robots make decisions.

- **Variables:** Refers to a storage space in memory that can hold value and can be stored and changed in a computer program. A variable changing can depend on either conditions or the information given to the program. Variable types can be expressed as characters, character strings, numeric values, memory addresses, and even objects. In robotics, variables are used as places to store values (i.e., sensor readings).

follow in a sequence of steps to achieve a goal. That process is likened to both a well detailed flowchart and code (in a specific programming language).

Practicing coding will help students understand that coding isn't complicated when they learn how to think logically and in steps. Getting students started by writing simple programs will teach them how to give computers instructions, how computers actually work, and that good coders aren't vague and don't skip steps. They will also understand that the code they write is processed (translated) by a compiler into machine language for execution. An added bonus for students learning to write code when programming robots is that they get to see how their code manipulates the most critical movements in real time.

For students new to coding, I recommend starting with a visual programming language (VPL), which allows them to describe their algorithms using illustrations and lets coders describe the process in terms that make sense to them.

Some popular VPLs are:

- Scratch, ScratchJr

- Blockly

- Ardublock (block programming language for Arduino)

- ROBOLAB (programming language for LEGO Robotics)

- ROBOTC (graphical for VEX Robotics)

- LabVIEW (National Instruments)

Although there are several ways to get students started in coding, I highly recommend your class participate in an Hour of Code (HOC). For getting started with an HOC visit Code.org for free access to a plethora of unique and fun coding activities.

PRO TIP

Presenting FTW!

Requiring students to present their work publicly is an excellent technique for engaging and instilling in them the importance of the testing process for discussing and showcasing high-quality robotics work.

Step 4: Test it (for debugging).

Testing in programming is a critical process used to determine the quality of a program and find bugs (problems). A debugger program is a program that assists in both detecting and correcting errors in your program's code. In robotics a debugger is used to control program flow and monitor variables.

As a college intern, I was first introduced to testing and debugging ActiveX Controls in the Visual Basic programming language. Although testing has different levels and will determine if programs work or don't, working to find bugs for the software developers to correct was very powerful in helping me understand the quality of the programs I used every day and also the importance of updating them regularly.

Last Word on Programming

For students who have already practiced coding using a VPL and either have or are mastering foundational programming principles, the next step is to get them coding in an industry sought-after programming language such as JavaScript, Python, Pearl, or C++. Luckily, programming a robot such as the VEX EDR (see the beginning of this chapter) gives them an introduction to this valuable learning experience. Students programming the VEX EDR learn to use the ROBOTC, C-based programming language and can see the effects of the code they write in real time by solving problems using the engineering design process.

RESOURCE

Programming and Coding Made Easy

ISTE: *Computer Programming in Four Steps* (bit.ly/2KUzMg2)

 Step-by step process for teaching programming.

Edutopia: *How to Get Started Teaching Coding* (edut.to/34BEnM3)

A three-step plan to help teachers in any subject and grade teach the foundations of coding.

PART 2

Robotics in the Content Areas

This section provides examples of successfully teaching with educational robotics through discussion of case studies and teacher testimonies. It also specifies the use of robotics, computational thinking (CT), programming, and aspects of computer science (CS) in the four content areas of English language arts (ELA), mathematics, science, and social studies. Additionally, this section specifies the significant content and skills that are pertinent to each of the areas, with alignment to CT and programming robots. The activities introduced in this section will provide teachers from the multiple disciplines precise ideas for teaching the new material from the perspective of their subject area. This section also comes complete with alignment to multiple standards, tips for teaching with evidence-based strategies, a lesson plan, and lots of access to curriculum from multiple reputable sources. The chapters in this section will explore:

- **Four teacher examples**
- **Robotics in ELA**
- **Robotics in mathematics**
- **Importance of science in today's schools and robotics in science**
- **Robotics in social studies**

6

Evidence for Robotics in the Classroom

A lot of work has been done by creators and developers of educational robotics and curriculum—which has made it possible for teachers to teach robotics and researchers to evaluate their use. Researchers obtain empirical evidence through experimentation or observation. Although researchers need to gather empirical evidence when learning about a topic that they are studying, classroom practitioners can benefit significantly from teacher success stories and step by step how-to blogs and articles.

For this chapter, the aim is to honor both the researcher and the teacher practitioner. Therefore, the provided evidence relates to both.

Empirical Evidence for Educational Robotics in the Classroom

Research tells us that constructivism and constructionism are the two leading theories that inform learning with educational robotics (ER). This is one of the main reasons why two of the chapters in the final section of this book focus on constructivism and evidence-based strategies (including PBL) for teaching and learning the content in this book.

Piaget made the argument that children construct knowledge by manipulating artifacts (Piaget, 1974). Not long afterward, his student Seymour Papert developed constructionism, his own theory based on Piaget's notion of constructivism, by making the case that knowledge construction happens best in contexts where learners consciously engage in constructing an artifact publicly, whether a sandcastle or a technological artifact (Papert, 1980).

Robotics strongly correlates to the constructionism theory in terms of assisting students with developing constructions that are tangible to others by viewing and through critique. Again, PBL works here for its inclusion of the "public product" as a significant event in the transferring of learning. It is also important to note that in the educational context, constructivism is more cognitive and constructionism is more physical.

Studies on Robotics in the Classroom

In a recent article by Sisman & Kucuk (2019), educational robotics was found to be an important learning tool because, when implemented correctly, learning the science of robotics provides learners an environment conducive to active learning and facilitates acquiring valuable 21st-century skills. Although the participants in the study were preservice teachers, the article struck a chord with me because it correlates to my own research (Valenzuela, 2019) aimed at improving teacher preparation for teaching computational thinking and computer science. It also provides the most up-to-date literature review on using constructivism and constructionism methods to help K–12 students create cross-curricular connections by learning robotics. According to the article:

> Papert was the first educational researcher to use the earliest implementations of Logo in allowing students to build a machine out of Lego pieces and to write a program to control the machine (Resnick, Ocko, & Papert, 1988). Since then, his studies using ER have become a popular topic (Goldman, Eguchi, & Sklar, 2004). ER can be a great tool for students to use in constructionist learning experiences (Alimisis, 2013; Mubin, Stevens, Shahid, Al Mahmud, & Dong, 2013). In addition, students have an opportunity to learn and utilize programming languages and receive immediate feedback. As stated by Papert: "Given a good programming language, I see children struggling to make a program

work in a way that they seldom sweat at their paper-and-pencil mathematics" (Papert, 1999, p 4). Therefore, ER activities may be beneficial
for improving the STEM skills of students. There are several studies in
which ER has been used in other fields such as mathematics (Hussain,
Lindh, & Shukur, 2006), science (Barak & Zadok, 2009), engineering (Hobbs, Perova, Rogers, & Verner, 2007), and physics education
(Williams, Ma, Prejean, Ford, & Lai, 2007; Martinez Ortiz, 2011) at all
education levels. (p. 510–511)

There is a need for more empirical studies on the effects of using ER with students.
With the advent of AI and CS4All, various grant funding opportunities will no
doubt result in more in-depth and long-term studies.

Robotics in the Classroom—Teacher Examples

Teachers looking to begin incorporating computational thinking and robotics in
their classroom can benefit from reading accounts of successful uses. This chapter
highlights examples from teachers who have successfully done so using a variety of
edtech. Teachers can read other accounts of teachers' experiences with robotics on
the EdTechTeacher blog (edtechteacher.org/blog).

Robots in Elementary Classrooms

Curriculum supervisor and a demonstration teacher Courtney Pepe of Jersey City,
New Jersey described in an EdTechTeacher blog post (2018) how elementary school
teachers at A. Harry Moore School used robots in several content areas, including
language arts and humanities. Here are two examples of how teachers used robots
to teach lessons in ELA and social studies.

USING SPHERO ROBOTS FOR READING COMPREHENSION In this lesson, Pepe
observes a teacher using a Sphero SPRK robot to assist students with their reading
and writing and speaking and listening skills, as well as skills in the 4Cs. Here she
describes in detail how this was done.

> The teacher read the story to the students as a traditional table activity.
> After they finished, the teacher moved the class to a more open space
> in the classroom. The teacher placed a SPRK robot on the ground and
> paired it with an iPad via Bluetooth. Also, the teacher had various
> objects set up on the floor that related to the story: seashells, sand,

grape juice, red sprinkles, and other objects. Next, the teacher began to ask a series of reading comprehension questions about the story, and the students took turns using the iPad to drive the SPRK robot to different objects in the room based upon the question that the teacher asked. An example of a question would be, "if you give the cat a cupcake" what will he ask to go with it?" As the teacher posed the question, the student drove the robot to the correct object (in this case, red sprinkles). Not only was this a great use of robotics to support reading comprehension but it also allowed the young students to practice their speaking and listening skills. Additionally, this lesson combined 21st skills—critical thinking, collaboration, and creativity—with a key subject using the three R's of reading, writing, and arithmetic plus media and technology.

USING BLUE-BOTS TO TEACH SOCIAL STUDIES   Blue-Bot is a Bluetooth-programmable robot that typically comes in a class pack. In this lesson, Pepe describes a teacher using Blue-Bots to help students with reading maps, programming, and critical thinking.

In this lesson, the students were learning about a "sense of place" because they were exploring the relationship between all of their home addresses in Jersey City, New Jersey. The teacher organized a map of Jersey City on a table with the home addresses of every student in the class. The first student had the Blue-Bot at the school and was given the challenge to successfully program the Blue-Bot so it would move to the student's home address as it was positioned on the map. Then, the second student coded the Blue-Bot to move from the home of the first student to the second student's address on the map, and so on. Not only was the lesson aligned to the New Jersey social studies standards, but it allowed the learners to think critically and solve problems that are steeped in real-life content.

Courtney documents this and other classroom projects using various edtech tools in her blog post.

RESOURCE

Examples of Robotics in the Classroom

Edtech Teacher: *Robotics in Elementary Classrooms, by Courtney Pepe* (bit.ly/2yf44Uz)

Robots in Middle School Classrooms

Kerry Zinkiewich is a blended learning and instructional technologies consultant. She is also a Technology Enabled Learning and Teaching Contact for the Kawartha Pine Ridge District School Board. She has years of experience overseeing the success of robotics in connecting curriculum to meaningful learning. Here Zinkiewich describes some of the ways her middle school teachers use robotics across the curriculum.

> It is a very good day when school is fun, but job one for all teachers and learners is to connect that fun with the fundamentals of the curriculum. Where, exactly, do coding and robotics fit into what schools are charged with teaching?
>
> Here is a start: Robotics students and teachers are making connections in math to spatial sense, patterning and problem-solving, reasoning, and proving process. In social studies, there are connections to mapping and in language, to reading a new language and procedural writing.
>
> "Teachers are starting to see how different robotics kits like Lego Mindstorm, Lego WeDo, and Vex can not only grab student attention but also help them learn concepts required from the curriculum in deep, meaningful ways," Zinkiewich says.
>
> One seventh grade classroom used the Vex IQ kits to reinforce the Cartesian plane by having students program the robots to move to various locations along the X and Y axes. In primary classrooms, students use the Lego WeDo kits to explore the various ways machines move, and to link the characters they build and program to story writing.
>
> Zinkiewich is also is excited by the creative way teachers are approaching the curriculum. It is no longer a series of skills to check off.
>
> "If we truly want our students to learn deeply, we need to consider the curriculum differently and bring students' interests and questions into the planning process. Robotics and coding supports that happening."

Technology teacher Trevor Takayama of Amherst, Massachusetts had a similar success story with one of his middle schoolers. Here Takayama describes the transformative effect building a robot had on a struggling student he calls J.

J had an aide every day because learning in the classroom was such a hardship for him. There was one exception—he loved technology class. If only, the young boy wished out loud, this exciting time could be more than just 40 minutes once a week.

One day, during an elective makerspace time with Takayama, he built a fully-functioning robot from only a few parts with a Lego EV3 kit in one class. He asked Takayama to please save it for him until next time.

The following week, his teacher gave J his own iPad mini and demonstrated how to use the Lego Commander app to connect to and control his robot—which the child named "Bob." When the next two classes met, J was no longer the struggler but the center of positive attention from his classmates on his "awesome creation" as he drove the robot down the hallway.

J is one of Takayama's favorite success stories. "When students free build or free play with robots, you can really see them being scientists," Takayama says. "They love to test things out, push the boundaries of the programming and try out the cool new toys. It's fascinating to see what they can come up with; each student does something different, and teachers usually learn a thing or two from them."

To learn more about the teacher's accounts, please read the ISTE blog by Gail Marshall. You can also glean insights into my practice using Sphero robots and littleBits in tandem with computational thinking in the Tech & Learning blog by Sascha Zuger.

RESOURCE

Examples of Robotics in K-8 Classrooms

ISTE: *Robotics in K–8 Classrooms, by Gail Marshall* (bit.ly/2Mp7Ov1) Blog post describing the

 role of robotics in connecting curriculum to deep, meaningful learning.

Tech & Learning: *Robotics in the Classroom, by Sascha Zuger* (bit.ly/2SIAjN2) Blog post describing how one teacher taught students how to build and program their own game designs in tandem with

computational thinking using the Sphero Bolt and littleBits Code Kit.

Robotics in ELA

When we think of literacy in the K–12 system, we typically think of reading and writing and the ability to communicate with others (i.e., speaking and listening). However, to fully develop technologically literate graduates, schools need to expand how literacy is viewed, used, and taught. According to the National Council of Teachers of English (2013), as society and technology change, so does literacy. Because technology has increased the intensity and complexity of literate environments, the 21st century demands that a literate person possess a wide range of abilities and competencies, and many literacies.

Moreover, the National Council of Teachers of English expresses that 21st-century literacy is defined as the ability to:

- Develop proficiency and fluency with the tools of technology;

- Build intentional cross-cultural connections and relationships with others to pose and solve problems collaboratively and strengthen independent thought;

- Design and share information for global communities to meet a variety of purposes;

- Manage, analyze, and synthesize multiple streams of simultaneous information; and,

- Create, critique, analyze, and evaluate multimedia texts (NCTE, 2013).

If the use of technology (namely in computer science) has changed the use of literacy, one has to wonder what schools have done to integrate computational thinking, programming, and coding in ELA classes and across the curriculum? It seems the better question to ask is, what can we do now?

Robotics an Entry to 21st Century Learning in ELA

Even though many ELA teachers may not initially see the value of covering how artificial intelligence and engineering automation works in their classrooms, my 15 years in education as both a teacher and instructional coach has informed me that lessons using robotics go beyond designing and programming and greatly enhance students' literacy competency. This is a natural byproduct because neither STEM nor computer science can be taught well without literacy.

It is important for ELA teachers to understand that teaching with robotics does not mean eliminating your entire curriculum or having to teach robotics for the entire school year. However, it does mean teaching your required ELA topics in ways that help students develop 21st-century skills. For example, reading (nonfiction informational text), writing, speaking, and listening are recurring strands in the English Language Arts Common Core State Standards that can easily be woven into all K–12 content, including lessons in robotics. These literacy standards are broad and have many learning objectives that educators should organize, introduce, and revisit as needed with students during every robotics design challenge.

When planning your robotics lessons, identify the specific ELA skills you want to reinforce, including informational writing, correct grammar, editing, sentence structure, paragraphing, applying knowledge of appropriate reference, speaking and listening, and critical thinking. Moreover, by focusing on the areas your students struggle with most, they will be able to improve their literacy skills over time through consistent practice.

Robotics and Literature

School-age children have a lot more content at their fingertips, are reading more than ever, and coming of age in a digitally advanced environment. They require the types of literary activities that will cause them to make meaningful and relevant connections to the world around them. As ELA teachers (and we all need to teach ELA), we need to remember that self-discovery is not easy and will not occur because our students like and comment on countless Instagram posts or Snapchats daily. Instead, we need to engage and coach them through activities that teach them to process and reflect on what they read in real time. If structured correctly, robotics can be a helpful scaffold for unpacking some of the common themes in literature.

Simple ways robotics can be used to enhance a literature lesson can include:

- Helping students make connections between writing with correct grammar and coding with proper syntax when programming robots.

- Representing the journey of literary characters through programmed robots.

- Helping a character in the story solve a problem (such as travel a specific distance, uses gears strategically to navigate through or around difficult terrain, or uss sensors as an alert of upcoming danger) by having students think analytically and design a robot (or computational artifact) that performs a specific function(s).

- Establishing empathy by having students program robots that can traverse difficult passages similar to those encountered by characters in literature.

Documenting the Process in a Design Journal

When working on robotics, it's essential for your students to document every step of the design process. Doing so consistently will develop their expertise in reading, writing, and expressing their ideas. Be sure to include frequent opportunities for students to document in an engineering design notebook or design journal.

In the real world, both designers and engineers use a design notebook to keep a log of their design projects from beginning to end. In it, they record their research, findings, observations, idea brainstorms, drawings, reflections, and new questions that they encounter throughout the design process. As keeping a journal is just as important as a finished product, ELA teachers can easily leverage it for helping their students with mastering reading and writing critically over time.

A good practice is to have students learn the rules and guidelines for logging in their design journals and to create the following the sections:

- Table of contents
- About the team
- Design Process: The challenge
- Design Process: Brainstorming
- Design Process: Select Approach
- Project management and timeline

Use Literacy Rubrics

When students are working in their design journals, it is good practice to have them use a rubric that is carefully aligned to ELA standards and that engages them in meaningful work (the robotics curriculum) so that you can be more intentional in your small group instruction and scaffolding. This will help in meeting them where they are regarding their literacy skills and assist with moving them forward. Moreover, students will be able to assess their own writing portions of the design process and develop literacy mastery at their own pace.

It is important to note that students will *not* become expert readers and writers in one design challenge. Although practice will not make perfect, it does make better, but only when it is consistent. Therefore, I recommend including the design journal and rubric in multiple design challenges involving robotics. You should also view design journal entries from challenge to challenge as both pre- and post-assessments and a measure of what your learners are able to do before instruction. This data from the journals should also be used to tailor your next steps to their actual needs and at the end of the lesson/unit in order to measure their growth and to reflect on your practice.

Be sure to design or seek out rubrics that clearly connect the reading and writing tasks students perform to your ELA standards. For example, use rubrics that guide elementary grade students in preparing journal entries that will help you determine their proficiency levels for being able to read and analyze nonfiction text, summarize information, and in writing an informational text. Students in middle school will additionally study nonfiction research methods and research-based argumentative writing. Therefore, the rubrics you use should be carefully crafted to guide them through determining main ideas and supporting details as they plan, draft, and revise essays, reports, or more complex journal entries. Table 7.1 shares an example rubric for an engineering design notebook.

Engineering Notebook

	EXCEPTIONAL 40 POINTS	GOOD 30 POINTS	FAIR 20 POINTS	NEEDS IMPROVEMENT 10 POINTS
Table of Contents	Table of contents accurately represents all of the entries in the notebook. Page numbers, titles, and dates are listed for each entry.	Table of contents represents most of the entries in the notebook. Page numbers, titles, and dates are occasionally missing. Entries are fairly neat and legible.	Table of contents has only occasional entries. Page numbers and/or dates are missing. Entries are barely legible.	No table of contents exists/ No entries in the table of contents.
Page Titles/ Objective	Page titles are accurately displayed at the top of each page. Titles clearly identify content of each page. Objective clearly written and dated. Entries are neat and legible.	Page titles are displayed at the top of each page but are occasionally missing/ inaccurate. Objective fairly clear and dated, however it could use more detail. Entries are fairly neat and legible.	An attempt at page titles is present but inaccurate. Frequent omissions occur. Objective is weak and missing most of the details. Dates may be missing. Entries are barely legible.	Page titles are missing. Objective is missing. Not dated.
Notebook Entries	All entries are consistently done in permanent blue or black ink. All entries, figures, and calculation are labeled clearly and consistently. Labels and diagram titles are printed and dated.	Most entries are done in permanent blue or black ink. Most entries, figures, and calculations are labeled. Labels and diagram titles are printed and dated. Occasional errors are evident.	Entries are frequently done in pencil and only occasionally done in permanent ink. An attempt at labeling entries, figures, and calculations is evident. Dates are inconsistently listed at the beginning of entries, if at all.	Entries are always done in pencil. No attempt is evident at dating entries and diagram titles.
Added Items	Items added to the notebook are permanently affixed to a page. Signature or initials are written in ink over the edge of the item.	Items added to the notebook are permanently affixed to a page. Signature or initials are missing over the edge of the item.	Items added to the notebook are permanently affixed, but are done so sloppily and with little care.	Items are not permanently affixed to the notebook OR items are done sloppily.
Mistakes/ Unused Space	Mistakes and errors are consistently lined out, initialed, and corrected. Unused space is consistently X'ed or lined out and a signature is present.	Mistakes and errors are lined out, initialed, and corrected. Unused space is X'ed or lined out and a signature is present. Occasional errors of omission are present.	Mistakes and errors are inconsistently or improperly lined out, initialed, and corrected. Unused space is occasionally X'ed or lined out and a signature is sometimes present. Errors of omission are frequent.	Clear evidence exists where items have been erased or scribbled out. Unused space is evident without being X'ed or lined out.
Pages Signed, Dated, and Witnessed	Pages are consistently signed and dated by the designer. Witness signatures and dates are also consistently displayed. No errors are evident.	Pages are signed and dated by the designer and witness. Occasionally errors of omission by the designer or witness are present.	Some evidence exists that signatures have been attempted by both the designer and witness. Frequent lapses and errors of omission are present.	No evidence is present that either the designer or a witness has signed and dated pages.

Table 7.1: Engineering Notebook rubric. Adapted from RCampus—an excellent source for educators to use for creating and sharing assessment tools (rcampus.com/index.cfm).

Pick the Right Tool for Your ELA Classroom

When choosing the right tool for you and your classroom, make sure to explore your options and remember to match your and your students' skill level with technology and edtech while also balancing the demands of your ELA curriculum. Incorporating a new robotics tool does not mean that we are no longer teaching ELA, nor do we abandon our best instructional strategies and practices for enhancing student learning.

 ELA Resources for Robotics Lessons and Curriculum

RESOURCE	DESCRIPTION	ACCESS
Terrapin Tools for Thinking *Bee-Bot Curriculum*	Bee-Bots are small, easy to program robots designed for young children.	(bit.ly/2YTHmh2)
Dexter Industries *GoPiGo3 Projects and Curriculum*	GoPiGo3 is a Raspberry Pi robot kit designed for introducing robotics.	(bit.ly/2OVocTh)
The LEGO Group *LEGO Education Lesson Plans*	LEGO creates physical and digital educational resources for all age groups.	(lego.build/2Kmu1L4)
LittleBits Education Curriculum	LittleBits invented the electronic building block and helps learners of all ages become designers and programmers.	(bit.ly/2I42qMq)
Wonder Workshop Curriculum	Wonder Workshop designs robots and lessons that can be integrated across the curriculum.	(bit.ly/2YUhdOV)

Moreover, when designing lessons that include robotics be sure to be intentional about the intended learning and your pacing and managing of activities, and do not skimp on the literacy needs of students. Useful strategies for preparing learners for the district and state-mandated tests while still engaging them in robotics may include incorporating the following into instruction:

- Product-driven reading and writing

- Mini lessons for modeling reading and writing strategies

- Text annotation for helping students make meaning and connections

- The "Readers and Writers Workshop" instructional model for focusing on the reading and writing of your students in practice

- Reflection for allowing learners to review and discuss their learning while making authentic connections

- Strategies that cause students to deepen their learning through analysis and interpretation

The good news is that makers of educational robots and robotics already include teacher-vetted lesson plans and activities that are aligned to the CCSS, the ISTE standards, CSTA standards, and the NGSS. I recommend visiting the websites of a few of the companies and exploring their lessons and curriculum to decide which activities would be a good match for your current ELA units before purchasing. This chapter shares several websites for you to check out along with QR codes for easy access.

Wonder Workshop

Introduction to Cue by Wonder Workshop

Lesson Plan
(bit.ly/2D0f4YM)

Overview

In pairs, students will examine the robot components of Cue to understand how the robot is able to move, display lights, and play sounds. Students will use the Cue app to program the robot's movements, lights, and sounds using both block-based programming and JavaScript.

Target Grades: 6–8

Duration

50–60 minutes

Objectives

STUDENTS WILL:

- Identify the Cue robot's motors, lights, microphones, and speakers.
- Use sequences to program Cue's movements, lights, and sounds.
- Use block-based and JavaScript languages to program Cue.

Vocabulary

App. An application that can be downloaded by a user(s)

Block programming. A method for teaching introductory coding dragging blocks of instructions

Lead programmer. A software engineer in charge of the software project(s)

Repeat block. Used to repeat a sequence of instructions until a specific condition is met

Robot. A machine that can replicate certain human movements and functions automatically

Materials, Resources, and Teacher Prep

DOWNLOADABLE MATERIALS:

- Cue Robot Components
- Evaluation Rubrics

OTHER SUPPLIES:

- Masking tape
- Cue robots (1 per group)
- Tablets or compatible devices (1 per group)
- Pencils
- Projector or interactive display with mirroring capability

Before the Lesson

- Install the **Wonder Workshop Cue** app on each device.
- Open the **Cue** app. Connect each robot by tapping the plus sign in the top right corner of the screen and then selecting the robot image. Name each robot by tapping **edit** and changing the name in the **name** box.
- Label each robot with its name using masking tape or labels.
- Fully charge the devices and robots.

- Provide each group with an email address and password to log into the **Cue** app.

- Ensure that there is reliable access to wireless internet in the classroom.

- Prepare a demo device with the **Wonder Workshop Cue** app by:

  - logging into the app

  - connecting a robot to the app

  - tapping on the **Code with Block & JavaScript** section of the app

  - tapping on the Challenges/Adventures section

  - completing the **Block** Challenge/Adventure called **Move** (You must complete the first Challenge/Adventure in order to create your own programs.)

Warm Up: Review

Programming with Blocks

1. Gauge students' experience using block-based programming languages by asking, "What have you programmed using blocks in Blockly, Code.org, or Scratch?" Sample responses might include "I programmed a dance with Dash using Blockly," "I programmed a video game in Code.org," or "I have no prior experience using coding blocks."

2. Ask, "What kinds of blocks did you use in your programs?" Sample responses might include: "I used a Repeat block so that Dash would dance forever," or "I used blocks so that the bird would move when the player clicked on the screen."

Direct Instruction

Cue Introduction

1. Make sure the Cue robot is not connected to the app. Then, turn on the robot.

- Wait for Cue to initiate the **Push** game or press the triangle/circle/square button on its head to begin play.

- Invite students to take turns playing the game.

2. Ask, "What do you notice about the robot? What can the robot do?"

- Sample response: "The robot can change lights, move its head, and move around."

- If students have used Dash before, have them identify the similarities and differences between Dash and Cue. (E.g., "All of Cue's buttons light up, whereas only one of Dash's buttons lights up.")

3. Project the Cue Robot Components slides. Refer to slides 1 and 2.

- Note how the colors of the dots next to each robot part's description match the colors of those parts on the robot image.

- Lead a discussion with students about which parts help the robot move (e.g., powered wheels, encoders, potentiometers, dual motors).

- In the same manner, discuss which parts help the robot display lights and play sounds (e.g., speaker, programmable LED, and buttons).

4. Navigate to the last two slides, where the dots are missing from each robot part's description.

- Select student volunteers to identify the location of each part on the Cue robot image and on the physical robot.

Quick Check:

- Which parts help the robot move?

- Which parts help the robot display lights?

Guided Practice

Introduction to Block Programming

1. Demonstrate how to create a new program in the **Code with Block & JavaScript** section.

- Project your device's screen and open the **Cue** app.

- Navigate to the **Code with Block & JavaScript** section.

- Tap on the **My Programs** section.

- For Chromebook/Microsoft platforms, select **New Program**.

- For iOS/Android platforms, select **Create New**.

2. Show students how to connect the app to the robot by tapping the plus sign at the top right and tapping the icon with the same name as the robot.

3. Drag out a few blocks from the **Actions** menu. Say, "With **Block**-based coding, you can program using blocks, just like in **Blockly** or **Code.org**."

   • Select student volunteers to create a program using three to four blocks. (Suggested blocks: **move distance**, **set light**, and/or **sound** blocks)

   • Run the program.

4. Say, "You can delete blocks by dragging them into trash can in the menu."

   • Model deleting a couple of blocks (See Figure 7.1).

5. Say, "With this app, you can turn your blocks into **JavaScript**! JavaScript is a text-based programming language that's used to create interactive effects within Web browsers." Then tap on the JavaScript icon at the top of the screen and tap the checkmark.

   • Have student volunteers add to the program by selecting additional lines of code from the **Actions** menu. Tap on the line icon at the top of the screen.

   • Run the program.

Figure 7.1: Deleting a block in Wonder Workshop Cue app.

6. Say, "You can also convert your program back into blocks." Then tap on the **Block** icon at the top of the screen.

- Have student volunteers point out the similarities and differences between the Block and JavaScript workspaces.

Quick Check

- How do you connect the app the to the robot? (You tap the plus sign in the top right corner of the screen.)

- How do you turn the blocks in your program into JavaScript? (You tap the JavaScript icon at the top center of the screen.)

Independent Practice

Have students work on the following activities in small groups (ideally two students per robot). Provide each group with a device and a robot.

Encourage students to share device and robot time. Have them establish and swap roles such as:

- **Lead Programmer**: Holds the device and manipulates the code

- **Robot Wrangler**: Retrieves and resets the robot after every program attempt

When students work together while coding, they're able to help each other identify mistakes and develop creative solutions.

Setting up Robots

1. Provide each group with their assigned account login information.

2. Have students log into the app.

- If it is the first time the app has been opened, have students walk through the lobby tutorial.

Block & JavaScript Challenges

1. Have students complete the following Challenges/Adventure in the **Code with Block & JavaScript** section:

- **Move** (blocks)
- Optional: **Move** (text)
- **Show** (blocks)
- *Optional:* **Show** (text)

2. After they complete the Challenges/Adventures, encourage students to try out the unlocked demos. Have them personalize one of the programs by changing its movements, lights, or sounds.

3. After they finish personalizing one of the example programs, have students:

   - Take a screenshot of their code.
   - Take a video of the Cue robot while the code is running.

Reflection and Wrap-Up

Student Presentations

1. Have student groups take turns sharing one of their programs with the class. Encourage them to:

   - Explain their design thinking. (E.g., "We changed the example program by adding recorded sounds so that the robot made different noises each time it moved forward.")

   - Share any obstacles and difficulties they overcame during the activity. (E.g., "We weren't sure how to record custom sounds in JavaScript, so we switched back to blocks to record the sounds.")

2. Encourage students to ask each other how they accomplished different objectives and give each other feedback on their programs. Possible questions/feedback include:

   - "Why did you (choose those sounds for your program)?"
   - "I like how you (recorded your own sounds)."
   - "What if you (changed the lights on the robot each time it moved)?"

Follow-up Questions/Discussion

- What are some of the blocks you can use to program Cue to move? (Sample response: "**Move distance, turn angle**, and **turn head** blocks.")

- Which parts of Cue can you program to show lights? (Sample response: "Cue's **ears**, **chest**, and **face**.")

- *Optional:* What are some differences between **Block** and **JavaScript** programming? (Sample response: "In JavaScript, when you want to use a command from the **Actions** menu, you need to start the line of code with the word 'actions'.")

- **Optional:* Which did you prefer using, Block or JavaScript programming? Why? (Sample response: "I liked using JavaScript because it was easier to customize colors.")

*Ask these questions after students have completed **Move** and **Show** in text.

Assessment

- Use Wonder Workshop's Evaluation Rubrics to review students' work and presentations (bit.ly/2pqoWrr).

Standards Addressed

Common Core

- **CCSS.ELA-LITERACY.RST.6-8.3:** Follow precisely a multistep procedure when carrying out experiments, taking measurements, or performing technical tasks.

- **CCSS.ELA-LITERACY.RST.6-8.4:** Determine the meaning of symbols, key terms, and other domain-specific words and phrases as they are used in a specific scientific or technical context relevant to grades 6–8 texts and topics.

Computer Science Teachers Association (CSTA)

- **1B-AP-10:** Create programs that include sequences, events, loops, and conditionals.

- **1B-AP-12:** Modify, remix, or incorporate portions of an existing program into one's own work, to develop something new or add more advanced features.

- **1B-AP-15:** Test and debug (identify and fix errors) a program or algorithm to ensure it runs as intended.

- **1B-AP-16:** Take on varying roles, with teacher guidance, when collaborating with peers during the design, implementation, and review stages of program development.

- **1B-AP-17:** Describe choices made during program development using code comments, presentations, and demonstrations.

- **1B-CS-01:** Describe how internal and external parts of computing devices function to form a system.

- **2-AP-12:** Design and iteratively develop programs that combine control structures, including nested loops and compound conditionals.

- **2-AP-13:** Decompose problems and subproblems into parts to facilitate the design, implementation, and review of programs.

- **2-AP-15:** Seek and incorporate feedback from team members and users to refine a solution that meets user needs.

- **2-AP-16:** Incorporate existing code, media, and libraries into original programs, and give attribution.

- **2-AP-17:** Systematically test and refine programs using a range of test cases.

ISTE Standards for Students

- **4d:** Exhibit a tolerance for ambiguity, perseverance and the capacity to work with open-ended problems.

- **5b:** Students formulate problem definitions suited for technology-assisted methods such as data analysis, abstract models and algorithmic thinking in exploring and finding solutions.

- **6b:** Create original works or responsibly repurpose or remix digital resources into new creations.

- **7c:** Contribute constructively to project teams, assuming various roles and responsibilities to work effectively toward a common goal.

Next Generation Science Standards (NGSS)

- **3-5-ETS1-2:** At whatever stage, communicating with peers about proposed solutions is an important part of the design process, and shared ideas can lead to improved designs.

- **MS-ETS1-3:** Analyze data from tests to determine similarities and differences among several design solutions to identify the best characteristics of each that can be combined into a new solution to better meet the criteria for success.

8

Robotics in Mathematics

In order for students to qualify for careers in STEM and to do well in the global economy, math and science must go hand and hand, and they need to come together in the classroom eventually. The key for math teachers is to teach what they have to cover "for the test" *and* do their very best to keep it "real-world." This can be accomplished with robotics by teaching students to engineer with computational thinking. According to the National Research Council (NRC) of the National Academy of Sciences:

> Although there are differences in how mathematics and computational thinking are applied in science and in engineering, mathematics often brings these two fields together by enabling engineers to apply the mathematical form of scientific theories and by enabling scientists to use powerful information technologies designed by engineers. Both kinds of professionals can thereby accomplish investigations and analyses and build complex models, which might otherwise be out of the question. (2012, p. 65)

Figure 8.1: Graphic with some of the habits of a systems thinker.
Source: Waters Foundation

Moreover, to possess the appropriate foundation for STEM, at minimum students must develop both algebraic thinking and engineering design skills. Algebraic thinking is first because it involves the ability to identify relationships, patterns, and functions between objects along with interrelationships between the variables that comprise said objects. Most importantly, schools should regard algebraic thinking as a journey that begins when learners begin to study mathematics for working with patterns in the early grades.

To truly understand how to build and design robots, students will need to utilize an engineering design process that provides both a systematic approach to solving engineering problems and the productive struggle needed for helping them construct knowledge. Accordingly, when working with robotics, math teachers will need to facilitate lessons and projects that correctly put mathematics in context within engineering design. Doing so will assist students with a deeper understanding of how math connects to engineering and develop systems thinking. For students, systems thinking enables them to analyze and comprehend how a system's parts (components) interconnect and how each is vital to the entire system(s) at large (see Figure 8.1). Engineering design will further be addressed in chapter 9 on science, however, the CCSS for math in this chapter are mapped to the NGSS.

Elementary: Using Robots to Make Algebraic and Geometric Connections and Develop Habits of Mind

Deeper learning and making connections to algebraic and geometric concepts that will effectively enable students' habits of mind (Boyes and Watts, 2009) will not come without our assistance, particularly in the case of our youngest learners. We need to highlight for them both the algebra and geometry concepts included in their robots and program solutions. As math teachers incorporating robotics into instruction, we should take time to determine which ideas from our curriculum frameworks (or curriculum), techniques, logic and which habits of mind correlate to activities with robots. Examples of this may include but are not limited to the following:

- Constructing paper robots for learning geometric shapes

- Understanding the power source and setting(s)

- Finding distance traveled

- Using the speed equation to define speed—speed = distance ÷ time

- Identifying and explaining a unit of speed

- Calculating speed of a robot moving in a straight line

- Calculating time to run a program (or mission)

- Applying their understanding of angles

- Deepening mastery of algebraic thinking skills

- Knowing the algebra involved when running the motors in robots with wheels

- Using reflection for metacognition

The examples above provide the insight that we do not have to wait for either middle or high school to provide our kids with real-world experiences that align with the standards. For the youngest children (K-2), pieces of algebraic language along with the learning shapes (geometry) already coincide with the expected rigor that is required there and continue in the other primary grade levels. Moreover, children who are afforded these opportunities become truly technologically literate and savvy, as a complement to their habits of mind. Habits of mind refers to the dispositions that students should learn to skillfully employ when faced with problems where solutions may not be immediately visible. Following are just a few of the 16 habits of mind as described by the Institute for Habits of Mind (habitsofmindinstitute.org). View the complete chart at bit.ly/38pCRPN.

Persisting: Stick to it! Persevering in task through to completion; remaining focused. Looking for ways to reach your goal when stuck. Not giving up.

Managing Impulsivity: Take your time! Thinking before acting; remaining calm, thoughtful, and deliberate.

Listening with understanding and empathy: Understand others! Devoting mental energy to another person's thoughts and ideas; Make an effort to perceive another's point of view and emotions.

Thinking flexibly: Look at it another way! Being able to change perspectives, generate alternatives, consider options.

Thinking about your thinking (Metacognition): Know your knowing! Being aware of your thoughts, strategies, feelings, and actions and their effects on others. (2017)

While young students are getting adjusted to either new robots or the concept of robotics, teachers will initially have to focus on combining play with work to bring out the right learning. Therefore, keep in mind that they will most likely not understand how and why their robots move and turn, so do not allow them to use arbitrary guess-and-check methods when programming. And although this type of play and guessing (tinkering) is often suitable when kids are building robots, this is not the case when programming because programs do not run well (or at all) with logical, syntax, or semantic errors. For this reason, I recommend explaining and teaching the importance of getting code right in their programs. Also, students may naturally rely on guessing and checking preprogrammed values or ones they enter for making their robot carry out intended functions. You will, therefore, have to help them be more precise by emphasizing calculations in their programs.

Helping students to refine their calculations and testing methods will enable them to learn skills that are the foundation for more advanced robotics in the later grades. Among these skills are:

- Developing reliable programming and building processes

- Ensuring that robots drive straight and correctly, travel with correct speed and distances, and turn on a correct angle

- Calculating appropriate wait time in programs for when robots need to travel specific distances

- Programming robots to precise grid coordinates and being able to plot the same points on a graph

- Programming robots to make both geometric pattern and shapes

- Using loops and conditional statements in code when programming

- Failing in order to succeed for persevering

Middle School: Ratios and Proportional Relationships

Students need to understand that ratios are everywhere and that they are already using them! For example, they get to choose the aspect ratio of their Instagram photos and use ratios to mix ingredients like milk and sugar with their favorite cereal. Moreover, students need to know how to determine if ratios are proportional by representing the same relationship. Unfortunately, many learners have only been introduced to this concept abstractly, such as writing ratios as fractions in order to reduce them to determine if the reduced fractions are the same and therefore proportional. Without a meaningful context for students, the intended learning in these types of activities may not be very retainable or readily accessible when needed.

It is therefore essential to provide students with the experiences they need to develop the algebraic reasoning skills needed for truly understanding ratios and proportional relationships. Because they will encounter ratios and proportion in every mathematics course they take from middle school into postsecondary, this is an excellent entry point for using robotics as a handy tool for teaching and learning. In the design of robots, proportional reasoning is key to understanding how movements are controlled, as well as the proportional relationships between the robot build, the values used to program it, and how it moves.

Moreover, using robotics to help learners understand rates, ratios, and proportions to develop algebraic ways of thinking is not an event but rather a process that occurs with repetition and time. This can be achieved by engaging them in lessons that include some of the following requirements and activities:

- Identify proportional relationship and gear ratios.

- Explain the proportional relationship of gear sizes and how it affects the distance their robot travels. Students can also create a graph to show this proportional relationship.

- Race robots and compare their speeds to explain what a point (x,y) on the graph of a proportional relationship means specific to the situation and also compute unit rates associated with ratios of fractions.

- Determine the proportional relationship of two quantities (i.e., speed of robots in a race). In a table, students will test for equivalent ratios and find a unit rate for a ratio that is defined by non-whole numbers. They will also learn to use an equation to represent a proportional relationship.

- Focus on distance, turning, and speed for direct proportional relationships to explore the difference between using a unit rate or scaling strategy to solve challenges.

- Solve proportional relationships that are direct and indirect to make their robots move either synchronously or asynchronously ("in synch" or "out of synch") with other robots.

- Calculate the circumference of wheels to determine the number of wheel rotations needed to program their robot's movement. For doing this, students must be aware that the distance traveled by a robot with wheels and the circumference of its wheels is proportional.

Learn the Math through Engineering

Lastly, I want to stress to math teachers who may not read the next chapter that incorporating the aforementioned items in the context of an engineering design challenge will provide their students valuable career skills in tandem with a systematized approach to solving difficult and complex problems. Moreover, aligning engineering practices to algebraic and geometric concepts will do wonders for developing the right-thinking skills and habits of mind. These skills also align with the K–12 standards for mathematical practice in the Common Core State Standards Initiative by allowing learners to make sense and solve problems, reason abstractly and quantitatively, model with mathematics, attend to precision, and communicate processes and results (2019).

Pick the Right Tool for Your Math Classroom

Even with the current trend of reduction and shortening of standardized testing throughout schools in the U.S., it appears that high stakes assessments in mathematics are not entirely going away yet. However, there is more encouragement for all educators to engage their students in real-world, hands-on learning and the use of performance-based assessments (Hilliard, 2015).

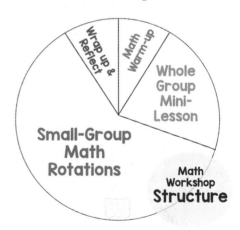

I say take advantage of this and fit in the right edtech (robots) and instructional approaches that are more problem- and project-based within your math classroom. Only vet tools that help students make logical connections to your math curriculum while still making time for weekly, biweekly, and benchmark assessments. And do not be afraid to put away your robots momentarily if students need to remediate essential

Figure 8.3: Math Workshop Structure. Source: Tunstall's Teaching Tidbits.

concepts and skills within your standards. Lastly, be sure to utilize instructional strategies like the "Math Workshop Model" (Matson, 2018) for providing the needed structure to your math stations. See figure 8.3 for a visual representation of Reagan Tunstall's structure for math workshops that you can adapt in your classroom.

 ## Math Resources for Robotics Lessons and Curriculum

RESOURCE	DESCRIPTION	ACCESS
Code.org *Robotics and Circuits*	Use robotics with these activities and make a tangible Hour of Code for students of any age! Some activities even offer a simulator so you can get started without any tools.	(code.org/learn/robotics)
Edison *10 Robotics Lessons*	These lessons have been tested with the Edison robot and a variety of other robots and have proven to be very successful.	(bit.ly/2ZvloQB)
The LEGO Group *LEGO Education Curriculum for Maths*	Make applied math more meaningful.	(lego.build/2PndeGv)
Ozobot Lesson Library	Find a variety of math-based STEAM lessons as well as other subjects.	(bit.ly/2IPwECq)
Sphero Edu	Host a large variety of math themed lessons and activities.	(bit.ly/2PuCxX5)

Sphero Lesson

Time, Speed, and Distance
Get Sphero to the Bank

 Sphero Lesson Plan for Mathematics
(bit.ly/36sHHuL)

Overview

Students will use Sphero to show that there is a linear relationship between time, speed, and distance in order to get Sphero to the bank. They will program Sphero to move at a particular speed for a particular amount of time and then measure how far it has gone. They will use division to find the relationships between time, speed, and distance. Finally, they will be given a challenge to take what they've learned and to have Sphero return to the place where it started.

The mathematics could be made to be more complex (for example, students could derive a formula where they predict the distance). Read through the student guide. At the start of the lesson, go over the concepts of time, speed, and distance.

Target Grades: Fourth and fifth, but can be adjusted for later grades as well.

Duration

50–60 minutes

Objectives

STUDENTS WILL:

- Create a one-line program that moves Sphero at a steady speed for a specified amount of time.

- Perform measurements to determine the distance traveled.

- Perform division to compare different measurements.

- Create a two-line program that moves Sphero to a certain position and then moves it back to where it started.

Materials Needed

Spheros are controlled via Bluetooth on either Apple (iPod, iPhone, or iPad) or Android devices. Ideally, you would do this lesson in groups of three or four students, each with their own Sphero and device. This lesson is designed for iPads, but other devices could be used. Here is what each group would need:

- iPad

- Sphero that has been fully charged

- Masking tape

- Tape measure

- Print-out of the worksheet (last page of teacher's guide)

- A flat clear path of at least 15 feet (and preferably not very slippery)

Figure 8.4: Plan your route.

Activities

Part 1: Plan your route.

A course has been laid out for you. Before using Sphero, you must first take accurate measurements to make certain you know where you are going. Use a measuring tool such as a ruler, yardstick, or tape measure. Measure the course Sphero needs to travel and create a diagram on a sheet of paper. See figure 8.4 for a sample route.

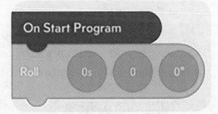

Figure 8.5: Using Roll command.

Part 2: Calculate the speed of Sphero.

- Set Sphero's speed.

- Because Sphero's speed is calculated as a percentage, we need to determine its feet-per-second.

  - Using block programming, start with the following settings in using the Roll command. See figure 8.5.

  - Start with 40% speed, 1 second with a heading of zero.

  - Measure distance.

Part 3: How far did Sphero travel?

Using your measurements, determine how far Sphero traveled in 1 second. Using your measurements, determine how far Sphero has to travel to make its first turn on the way to the bank.

Add a stop command.

Part 4: Time to make a turn.

Now that we know how fast Sphero is traveling, it needs to turn on its way to the bank. Set Sphero to stop and turn. Remember you need to change the heading of Sphero to make it all work. Measure how far it needs to travel to turn into the parking lot that will be your next stop.

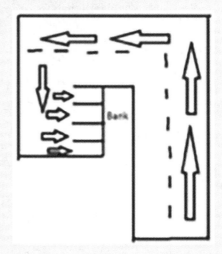

Figure 8.6: Top view of course to bank.

Part 5: Challenge

So far so good for Sphero. It now needs to enter the parking lot on the way to bank. Don't forget course headings and speed. Remember you may need to recalculate speed. See figure 8.6 for a view of the course to bank.

Part 6: Parking Sphero

It is now time to park Sphero in its parking spot. Remember to do it nice and gently.

Its speed may need to be adjusted. No one drives full speed into a parking spot.

Part 7: Congratulations!

Sphero made it into its parking spot! It can now get to the bank and cash its check at the bank.

Part 8: Extra Challenge

Try to reverse Sphero and get it back where it started from.

Standards Addressed

Common Core

The following Common Core Math Standards for 4th and 5th grade apply to this lesson:

- **CCSS.MATH.CONTENT.4.OA.C.5:** Generate and analyze patterns.

- **CCSS.MATH.CONTENT.4.MD.A.2:** Use the four operations to solve word problems involving distances, intervals of time, etc.

- **CCSS.MATH.CONTENT.4.OA.C.5:** Generate and analyze patterns.

- **CCSS.MATH.CONTENT.5.OA.B.3:** Analyze patterns and relationships.

- **CCSS.MATH.PRACTICE.MP1:** Make sense of problems and persevere in solving them.

- **CCSS.MATH.PRACTICE.MP2:** Reason abstractly and quantitatively.

- **CCSS.MATH.PRACTICE.MP4:** Model with mathematics.

- **CCSS.MATH.PRACTICE.MP8:** Look for and express regularity in repeated reasoning.

CSTA K-12 Computer Science Standards

- **1B-AP-08:** Compare and refine multiple algorithms for the same task and determine which is the most appropriate.

- **1B-AP-09:** Create programs that use variables to store and modify data.

- **1B-AP-10:** Create programs that include sequences, events, loops, and conditionals.

- **1B-AP-12:** Modify, remix, or incorporate portions of an existing program into one's own work, to develop something new or add more advanced features.

ISTE Standards for Students

- **1.a.** Articulate and set personal learning goals, develop strategies leveraging technology to achieve them and reflect on the learning process itself to improve learning outcomes.

- **3.d.** Build knowledge by actively exploring real-world issues and problems, developing ideas and theories and pursuing answers and solutions.

- **4.a.** Build knowledge by actively exploring real-world issues and problems, developing ideas and theories and pursuing answers and solutions.

- **5.a.** Formulate problem definitions suited for technology-assisted methods such as data analysis, abstract models and algorithmic thinking in exploring and finding solutions.

- **5.c.** Break problems into component parts, extract key information, and develop descriptive models to understand complex systems or facilitate problem-solving.

NGSS Science and Engineering Practices

- **3-5-ETS1-2.** Generate and compare multiple possible solutions to a problem based on how well each is likely to meet the criteria and constraints of the problem.

- **MS-ETS1-3:** Analyze data from tests to determine similarities and differences among several design solutions to identify the best characteristics of each that can be combined into a new solution to better meet the criteria for success.

CHAPTER 9

Science in Schools

S cience is a multifaceted subject and is the class in schools where both scientific inquiry and engineering design (STEM learning) can truly come to life for many children with tools like those used in robotics. Unfortunately, science does not always get the emphasis it truly needs in either schools or the lives of children in K-8, particularly in the early years. As a large portion of my work involves working with teachers, I am alarmed when they tell me that science often gets minimal time in many K-5 schools. When I ask why, I am always informed that everything in their school must take a backseat to mandated reading and math time, testing, and remediation for more testing.

That children in the primary grades are not getting enough science time is actually not a new problem, and there is empirical research to back up the claim. In a study conducted by WestEd in 2011, a survey of 300 elementary schools throughout 451 school districts in California public schools revealed that forty percent of K-5 teachers said they were only able to dedicate an hour or less to teaching science weekly. Equally alarming, about 85 percent of those elementary teachers reported not receiving any science-based professional development during the three previous years (Dorph et. al., 2011). The study revealed that the culprits once again are the pressure to focus on standardized testing for ELA and math, and teachers feeling ill prepared to teach science. A national survey inclusive of both science and mathematics education conducted by a research firm in North Carolina reported similar findings (Banilower et. al., 2013).

> Although there is an argument that young children do not have the capacity to learn real science, there is a consensus among some cognitive scientists that disagree and appeal with the following statement: All young children have the intellectual capability to learn science. Even when they enter school, young children have rich knowledge of the natural world, demonstrate causal reasoning, and are able to discriminate between reliable and unreliable sources of knowledge. In other words, children come to school with the cognitive capacity to engage in serious ways with the enterprise of science. (NRC, 2007)

Perhaps if more emphasis were placed on prioritizing science education at both the federal and state levels, then our country would be receiving a better return on our investment in STEM education (Groome, 2017). I say this because although STEM concepts can and are often applied in multiple classrooms and by many educational organizations, engineering design—the pedagogical approach for STEM education—lives within the NGSS framework for science. Moreover, when the NGSS was officially released in 2013, for the first time in K-12 education, the document elevated engineering design to the same level of scientific inquiry. And if we are truly preparing students in the STEM fields, with many teachers not having engineering backgrounds, effective teacher training in both science and engineering design needs to be the utmost priority.

Robotics in Science

Learning and understanding science is understanding the world around us. According to the NGSS website:

> Science—and therefore science education—is central to the lives of all Americans. A high-quality science education means that students will develop an in-depth understanding of content and develop key skills—communication, collaboration, inquiry, problem solving, and flexibility—that will serve them throughout their educational and professional lives. (2019)

Before jumping into robotics in science, I would like to touch on how the NGSS can be leveraged as a powerful tool for helping students understand science in the broader sense.

The NGSS framework (shown in Figure 9.1) is very powerful because it provides teachers three different yet essential dimensions for gradual but cohesive learning and understanding of science. The standards in the NGSS are written as performance expectations and the three dimensions join to form each of the performance expectations:

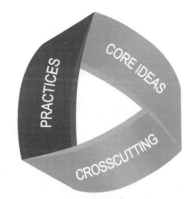

Figure 9.1: The Three Dimensions of Science Learning in the NGSS. Source: The NGSS website

1. **Disciplinary Core Ideas (DCIs)** are significant and core ideas in science that cut across multiple disciplines in both science and engineering.

2. **Science and Engineering Practices** describe how scientists investigate the natural world of plants and animals and what engineers do to design and construct systems in the physical world (or the designed world).

3. **Crosscutting Concepts** assists students with understanding how one branch of scientific knowledge connects to another. Awareness of crosscutting concepts is key to understanding the four domains of science found in the NGSS —Physical Science, Life Science, Earth and Space Science, and Engineering Design.

Learning parts of science with robotics can be very powerful because robotics can be applied to the practices of both scientists and engineers and therefore cut across multiple DCIs and help students connect some of the pertinent crosscutting concepts.

So, to best determine how we would like to use robotics in our science class, let us briefly illustrate the practices of scientists and engineers.

The purpose of the graphic in figure 9.2 is to demonstrate a side-by-side comparison of key components in the practices of scientists and engineers for helping you determine the best uses for your robotics lessons. However, it is important to note that both the NGSS (adopted by 22 states) and many science educators are moving away from the traditional scientific method as a linear process. It is also important to point out that not all of our students will do science as an experiment.

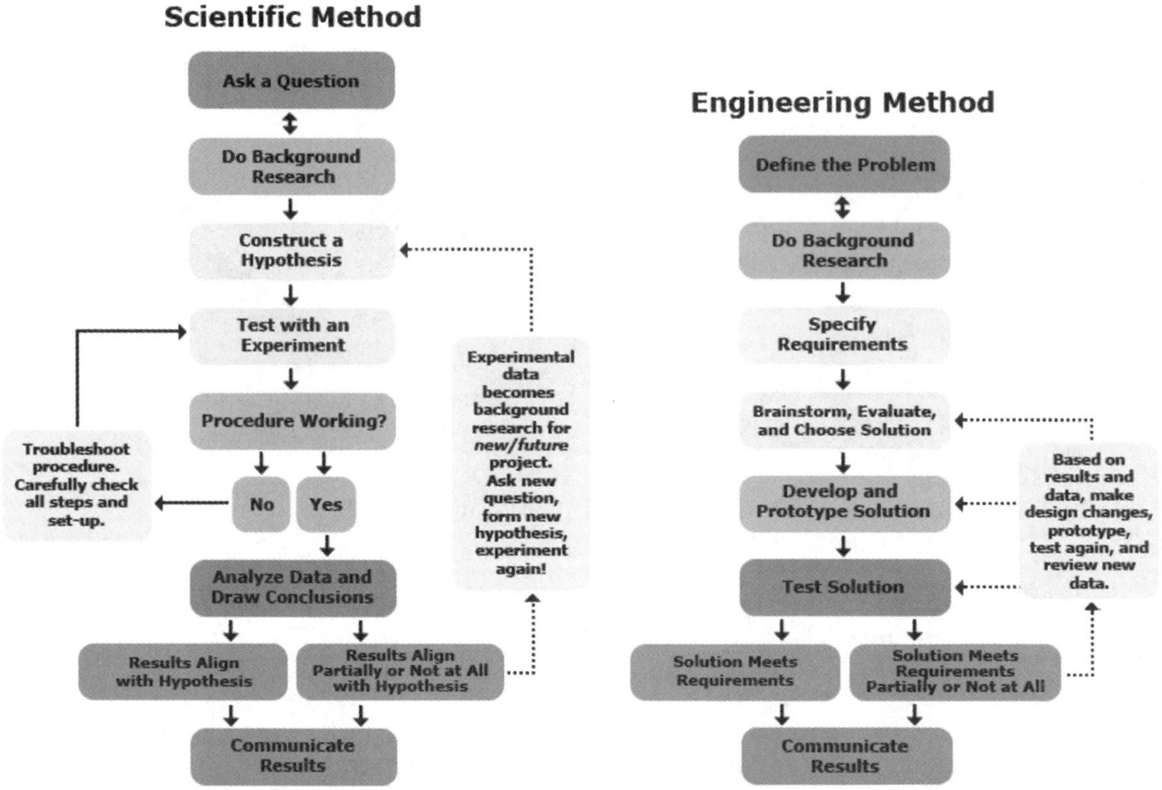

Figure 9.2: Comparing the Engineering Design Process and the Scientific Method. Source: Science Buddies

Why are there two processes in science and which do I choose?

Although at times the work of scientists and engineers does overlap, their contributions to humanity and their fields differ.

Traditionally, the scientific method is used by scientists for conducting experiments, observations, and measurements in the natural world. Procedures will vary between the inquiry fields, but the process is typically the same and is modified as needed (meaning not always applied rigidly or in sequence). The scientific method involves asking a question, making hypotheses, and obtaining predictions from them in the form of logical consequences. Scientists then carry out experiments or empirical observations based on the predictions to answer the question.

Many science educators are shying away from teaching the scientific method in rigid steps and are instead focusing on both the application and practice of science. The NGSS supports this style of inquiry-based learning with the eight practices identified in the framework for science and engineering practices that all students should know.

The work of engineers involves using the engineering design process to solve problems in the physical world. The process involves an engineer or a team of engineers working to identify a specific need, determining what is needed and by who, and then developing solutions for fulfilling the need.

As mentioned above, the work of scientists and engineers do overlap and at times, scientists do some engineering work and engineers often need to take scientific principles into account while designing solutions. However, today's scientists and engineers are spending a lot more of their time developing computer programs that help them process, transform, clean up, and obtain insights from the data they collected while working in the field. Quite a bit of work that is referred to as "CS" is achieved by engineering because essentially, programmers create and refine both physical and computational products.

If you are unsure where your lessons and projects should fall between science and engineering, no need to worry. Many engineering projects do and should use scientific principles. However, because we are going to be building robots and programming, let's follow the structure of the engineering design process.

Other Approaches to Design

For teachers who are not explicitly teaching engineering, having students employ other systematic approaches for measurement, observation, experiments (i.e., the scientific method), integration of the arts (for art and music), and design thinking will heighten their levels of cognition.

When educators structure their learning environments to include design and inquiry processes consistently, we increase the development of students who are both analytical and critical thinkers and with the power to innovate.

Although not every learner will become an artist, scientist, or engineer, by consistently using these practices, all students can understand how to solve problems, how systems work, how natural phenomena behave, and how effective use of technology and their subjects connect. Moreover, these skills have wide-ranging career and job applications, including technicians, operators, customer service representatives, or health and medical professionals in a career and technical education program.

Early Elementary: Using Robotics to Do Science

Students in elementary school are learning about the world as they experience it and how to make sense of it. They intuitively use the traditional five senses (sight, hearing, taste, smell, and touch) for sensory perception and rely on learning through their ears, eyes, and hands as well as by listening and observing adults and peers. In this stage of life, learners use these faculties and resources for drawing, molding, reading, mimicking, and for manipulating objects and numbers. Introducing robots in science class can support them to work through problems visually, physically, and to experiment and test the concepts they are learning.

Early science curriculum can be leveraged with robotics to help students do science within good structure(s) through the following activities:

- Applying computational thinking skills

- Designing, building, and programming robots to investigate solutions and solve problems

- Working in design teams to collaborate with others and share ideas to investigate, create, and test the best possible solutions

- Exploring real-world scientific questions in science topics ranging from earth science to physics.

- Developing hypotheses and testing them out.

- Conducting experiments

- Using reflection for metacognition, persevering

Grades 4–8: Using Robotics to Teach Physics

Learning physics through robotics can simplify and put into context the study of energy, motion, matter, electricity, and mechanics for the tech-savvy youth of today. Additionally, using robotics can speed up the learning curve of any student struggling to understand how their beloved devices actually work, along with the physics in the interaction of moving objects, and the simple science that makes motion sensors and touch screens possible.

Simply put, robotics is a learning tool (maybe even *the* learning tool) that brings order to the most inaccessible topics in physics, such as making sense of the role quantum mechanics plays in the development of AI-enhanced robots for creating some of the amazing things we use and see daily.

Examples of NGSS performance expectations that align with educational robotics include but are not limited to the following:

- **4-PS3-1:** Use evidence to construct an explanation relating the speed of an object to the energy of that object

- **4-PS3-2:** Make observations to provide evidence that energy can be transferred from place to place by sound, light, heat, and electric currents.

- **4-PS3-3:** Ask questions and predict outcomes about the changes in energy that occur when objects collide.

- **4-PS3-4:** Apply scientific principles to design, test, and refine a device that converts energy from one form to another.

- **MS-PS2-2:** Plan an investigation to provide evidence that the change in an object's motion depends on the sum of the forces on the object and the mass of the object.

- **MS-PS3-2:** Develop a model to describe that when the arrangement of objects interacting at a distance changes, different amounts of potential energy are stored in the system.

- **MS-ETS1-1:** Define the criteria and constraints of a design problem with sufficient precision to ensure a successful solution, taking into account relevant scientific principles and potential impacts on people and the natural environment that may limit possible solutions.

- **MS-ETS1-2:** Evaluate competing design solutions using a systematic process to determine how well they meet the criteria and constraints of the problem.

- **MS-ETS1-3:** Analyze data from tests to determine similarities and differences among several design solutions to identify the best characteristics of each that can be combined into a new solution to better meet the criteria for success.

- **MS-ETS1-4:** Develop a model to generate data for iterative testing and modification of a proposed object, tool, or process such that an optimal design can be achieved.

- **MS-PS2-1:** Apply Newton's third law to design a solution to a problem involving the motion of two colliding objects.

- **MS-PS3-5:** Construct, use, and present arguments to support the claim that when the kinetic energy of an object changes, energy is transferred to or from that object.

How Mathematics and Computational Thinking are Applied in Science

In science, both mathematics and computational thinking go hand-in-hand and should be applied in classrooms for representing physical variables and their relationships. In K–8 classrooms, this enhances and makes fun for students' statistical analysis, creating simulations, and deciding when to use qualitative versus quantitative data. Although this is often considered the hard stuff in school, when made fun with robotics tools, kids get the exposure they need to the real-world application of how mathematics is leveraged with computation for research. Not only do scientists and engineers apply these skills, but so do the companies who need a talent pool that is both grounded in the basics and dedicated to the continuous expansion of said skills.

According to the National Research Council (NRC) of the National Academy of Sciences:

> Although there are differences in how mathematics and computational thinking are applied in science and in engineering, mathematics often brings these two fields together by enabling engineers to apply the mathematical form of scientific theories and by enabling scientists to use powerful information technologies designed by engineers. Both kinds of professionals can thereby accomplish investigations and analyses and build complex models, which might otherwise be out of the question. (2012, p. 65)

The National Science Teachers Association (NSTA) has created a K–12 progression chart of how mathematics and computational thinking can be used in both science and engineering, along with the correlated performance expectations. Table 9.1 shares the progression for grades K–8. This is a helpful tool to use along with the Science Resources for Robotics Lessons and Curriculum section of this chapter.

Table 9.1 **Mathematics and Computational Thinking Progression Chart**

PRIMARY SCHOOL (K–2)	ELEMENTARY SCHOOL (3–5)	MIDDLE SCHOOL (6–8)
Mathematical and computational thinking in K–2 builds on prior experience and progresses to recognizing that mathematics can be used to describe the natural and designed world(s).	Mathematical and computational thinking in 3–5 builds on K–2 experiences and progresses to extending quantitative measurements to a variety of physical properties and using computation and mathematics to analyze data and compare alternative design solutions.	Mathematical and computational thinking in 6–8 builds on K–5 experiences and progresses to identifying patterns in large data sets and using mathematical concepts to support explanations and arguments.
		Decide when to use qualitative vs. quantitative data.
Use counting and numbers to identify and describe patterns in the natural and designed world(s).	Organize simple data sets to reveal patterns that suggest relationships.	Use digital tools (e.g., computers) to analyze very large data sets for patterns and trends.
Describe, measure, and/ or compare quantitative attributes of different objects and display the data using simple graphs.	Describe, measure, estimate, and/or graph quantities such as area, volume, weight, and time to address scientific and engineering questions and problems.	Use mathematical representations to describe and/or support scientific conclusions and design solutions.

Source: NSTA

Science Resources for Robotics Lessons and Curriculum

RESOURCE	DESCRIPTION	ACCESS
Carnegie Mellon Robotics Academy *Curriculum for STEM Excellence*	Use the motivational effects of robotics to excite students about STEM.	(bit.ly/2MkyvCN)
Exploring Robotics *STEM Pathways curriculum*	STEM, robotics, and coding curriculum.	(bit.ly/311VQMX)
Junk Drawer Robotics *Robotics Facilitator Resources*	Junk Drawer Robotics emphasizes different aspects of robotics while youth build their own robots and develop robotics knowledge and skills.	(bit.ly/2KhRStz)
Kinder Lab Robotics *Teacher materials*	Easy ways to integrate STEAM robotics into the existing curriculum.	(bit.ly/2KhRStz)
NASA: *The Robotics Alliance Project*	Explore the Educational Robotics Matrix.	(go.nasa.gov/2lgHuzp)

Pick the Right Tool for Your Science Classroom

This chapter focused a lot on truly having students learn and apply the practices of scientists and engineers, along with highlighting the appropriate performance expectations (standards) and approaches provided within the NGSS and supported by the NSTA and NRC. I did this because I did not feel the need to develop correlations between science, robotics, and computational thinking for you. The NGSS already does this exceptionally well and my only job here was to point you to where it is.

It is also important to note that the NGSS writing team included the U.S.'s top experts in K–12 science, students with disabilities, English language acquisition, curriculum, assessment alignment, and workforce development. These folks were selected based on recommendations from the NSTA, the Council of State Science Supervisors, and other reputable organizations. So, when picking the right tool for you, make sure to scan the curriculum associated with said tools for correlations to the performance expectations recommended in this chapter.

Lego Lesson

LEGO Object Detection

LEGO Lesson Plan for Science
(lego.build/32Zu83p)

Overview

In this interactive lesson, students learn to design ways to avoid accidents between vehicles and objects on the road. They will build a robot equipped with sensors and create code for testing various commands for safety.

Target Grades: 6-8

Duration

90-120 minutes

Objectives

- Students will learn CS fundamentals using drag and drop blocks.
- Students will design and construct a safe model of a vehicle for testing.

Vocabulary

Code. The set of instructions forming a computer program which is executed by a computer.

Sensors. Robotic sensors are used to estimate a robot's condition and environment.

Input. Any information or data sent to a computer for processing.

Output. Data generated by a computer.

Algorithm. A set of instructions designed to perform a specific task.

Pseudocode. A detailed yet readable description of what a computer program or algorithm must do, expressed in a formally-styled natural language rather than in a programming language.

Debug. The routine process of locating and removing computer program bugs, errors or abnormalities.

Logic. A computer programming paradigm in which program statements express facts and rules about problems within a system of formal logic.

Loops. In code, a sequence of instructions that is continually repeated until a certain condition is reached.

Materials, Resources, and Teacher Prep

- LEGO® MINDSTORMS Education EV3 core set

- LEGO MINDSTORMS EV3 Software or Programming app

- ROBOTC software (optional)

- Student worksheet (access at lego.build/30WaFAv)

- Assessment Rubrics (access at bit.ly/30WUB1g)

- Introduction to EV3 Coding Activities (access at bit.ly/2QAzFZn)

Connect (5 min)

Ignite a classroom discussion around the following questions:

- In what driving situations can a car hit an obstacle?

- What factors are crucial to be aware of in order to avoid collisions with obstacles?

- What causes traffic jams in high-density areas?

Allow the students to select the tool(s) they find most appropriate for capturing and sharing their ideas. Encourage them to document their thoughts using text, videos, images, sketchnotes, or another creative medium.

Direct Instruction --

Introduce the concept of sensors and what they are used for. Also introduce the digital EV3 Ultrasonic Sensor and how it generates sound waves and reads their echoes to detect and measure distance from objects.

Emphasize for students how the sensor can also send sound waves to work as sonar or listen for a sound wave that triggers the start of a program. Set up future open-ended projects by informing students that they could design a traffic-monitoring system and measure distances between vehicles, for instance. There is an opportunity to help students discover how the technology is used in everyday items such as automatic doors, cars, and manufacturing systems. Other features of the digital EV3 you can explain for students are:

- It measures distances between 1–250 cm (1–100 in.)
- It is accurate to +/- 1 cm (+/- 0.394 in.)
- Front illumination is constant while emitting and blinks while listening
- Returns True if other ultrasonic sound is recognized
- Auto-ID is built into the EV3 Software

Construct (30 min)

Build

Students will construct the Robot Educator base model and then add the Ultrasonic Sensor pointing forward.

A building instruction guide tutorial with pictures can be downloaded from bit.ly/2Z4v44N.

Testing

Have the students perform the following building check before they program their robots:

- Are the wires correctly connected from the motors to ports B and C?
- Are the wheels correctly installed?
- Are the wheels rotating freely?
- Are the wires correctly connected from the Ultrasonic Sensor to 4?

Program

Demonstrate the **Wait Block** and how to use it with the Ultrasonic Sensor.

Ask the students how they could make a program to detect any obstacles that might appear while the wheeled robot is moving forward (or backward).

Direct students to use the engineering design process and the algorithm design computational thinking element to provide steps and process.

Students will create a program that makes the robot stop at a given point based on a distance measured by the Ultrasonic Sensor.

Allow the students to select the tool(s) they find most appropriate for capturing and sharing their pseudocode. Encourage them to use text, videos, images, sketchnotes, or another creative medium.

Here is a possible program solution that you can use to support first time programmers. It requires the EV3 desktop app and can be downloaded from the link at the beginning of the lesson plan. FILENAME: CODING-05.EV3 (TAB: 1)

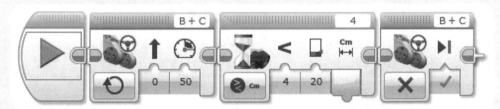

Figure 9.3: Simple Sample Program: Detect Objects and Stop.

Sample Program: Detect Objects and Stop (See figure 9.3)

- Start the program.
- Turn both motors on at speed 50.
- Wait for the Ultrasonic Sensor to detect an obstacle at a distance of less than 20 cm.
- Turn both motors off.

Note: Refer students to the Robot Educator Tutorials for further assistance. In the EV3 Software: Robot Educator > Basics > Stop at Object

Set Up

Before assigning the next task, make sure that you have marked the path the robots must follow and that there is enough space to complete the task. It is a good idea to have students work on a big table or the floor.

Have the students experiment with using the Ultrasonic Sensor to detect different objects. One of the objects can be a cuboid made of LEGO bricks.

Building instructions can be accessed by students at bit.ly/2HMrCWz

Contemplate (35 min)

On the road, when a driver sees an object, they slow their car down before coming to a full stop. Have the students program their robots with the same behavior.

If the Ultrasonic Sensor:

- Detects an object less than 10 cm away, make the robot stop
- Detects an object between 10 and 20 cm away, make the robot slow down
- Does not detect any object, continue to move at full speed

Here is a possible program solution that you can use to support first time programmers. It requires the EV3 desktop app and can be downloaded on the lesson link above. FILENAME: CODING-05.EV3 (Tab: 2)

Detect Objects and React (See figure 9.4)

1. Start the program.
2. Turn both motors on at speed 50.
3. IF the Ultrasonic Sensor detects an obstacle at a distance of less than 10 cm, turn both motors off.
4. ELSE
5. IF the Ultrasonic Sensor detects an obstacle at a distance of less than 20 cm, turn both motors on at speed 10.
6. ELSE
7. Turn both motors on at speed 50.
8. Repeat steps 3 to 7 forever.

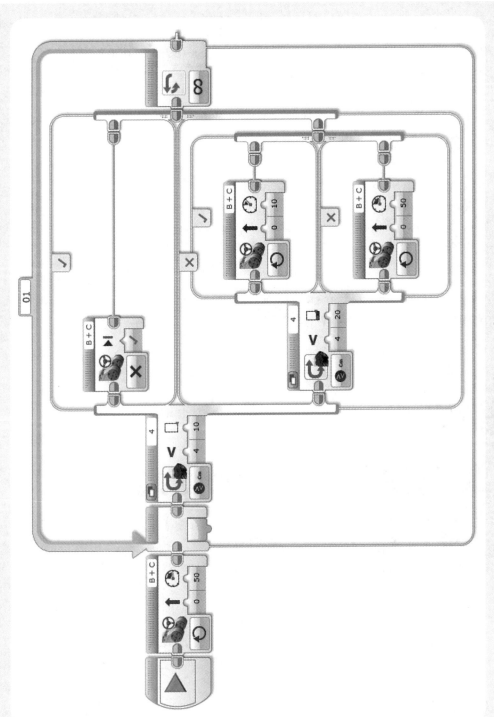

Figure 9.4: Detect objects and react.

Differentiation Option

Bring all the teams together. Tell the students to place their robots in a vertical line with varying amounts of space between them (just like cars in a traffic jam). Have them start their programs at the same time and watch what happens.

Ask the students to refine their programs so that all of the robots continue driving at the same speed with equal distances between them (like well-flowing traffic on a road).

Share

Allow the students to select the tool(s) they find most appropriate for capturing and sharing their creations, unique thinking, and learning process. Encourage them to use text, videos, images, sketchnotes, or another creative medium.

Discuss the concept of efficiency in programming.

How many variations did the group as a whole come up with? Compare the many possible solutions to the given problem.

Assessment Opportunity

Specific rubrics for assessing computational thinking skills can be found under "Assessment" or at bit.ly/30WUB1g. See Table 9.2 for a progression chart showing how mathematics and computational thinking can be used in both science and engineering in grades K–8.

Reflection and Wrap-Up (5–10 min)

What did we learn?

- What did we learn about sensors and their uses?

- If a problem is too hard, how does the engineering process and computational thinking help us?

- What are the various code blocks and what do they help us accomplish in our programs?

- How may I design my robot differently next time?

Table 9.2 **Algorithmic Thinking Rubrics**

	BRONZE	SILVER	GOLD	PLATINUM	NOTES
Describe the list of actions to program.	The student is unable to describe a list of actions.	With prompting, the student is able to describe a list of actions.	The student is able to describe a list of actions.	The student is able to create a detailed list of actions to help them develop their program.	
Describe how you have programmed your solution.	The student is unable to describe the program	With prompting, the student is able to describe the program.	The student is able to describe the program	The student is able to describe the program, providing extensive details about each component.	
Describe the programming principles used in your solution (e.g., output, inputs, events, loops, etc.)	The student is unable to describe the programming principles used in their solution.	With prompting, the student is able to describe the programming principles used in their solution.	The student is able to describe the programming principles used in their solution.	the student is able to describe, with extensive comprehension, the programming principles used in their solution.	

Source: NSTA

111

Standards Addressed

NGSS Science and Engineering Practices

- **MS-ETS1-1:** Define the criteria and constraints of a design problem with sufficient precision to ensure a successful solution, taking into account relevant scientific principles and potential impacts on people and the natural environment that may limit possible solutions.

- **MS-ETS1-2:** Evaluate competing design solutions using a systematic process to determine how well they meet the criteria and constraints of the problem.

- **MS-ETS1-3:** Analyze data from tests to determine similarities and differences among several design solutions to identify the best characteristics of each that can be combined into a new solution to better meet the criteria for success.

- **MS-ETS1-4:** Develop a model to generate data for iterative testing and modification of a proposed object, tool, or process such that an optimal design can be achieved.

CSTA K-12 Computer Science Standards

- **2-CS-01:** Recommend improvements to the design of computing devices, based on an analysis of how users interact with the devices.

- **2-DA-09:** Refine computational models based on the data they have generated

- **2-AP-10:** Use flowcharts and/or pseudocode to address complex problems as algorithms.

- **2-AP-12:** Design and iteratively develop programs that combine control structures, including nested loops and compound conditionals.

- **2-AP-13:** Decompose problems and subproblems into parts to facilitate the design, implementation, and review of programs.

- **2-AP-15:** Seek and incorporate feedback from team members and users to refine a solution that meets user needs.

- **2-AP-17:** Systematically test and refine programs using a range of test cases.

ISTE Standards for Students

- **1.a.** Articulate and set personal learning goals, develop strategies leveraging technology to achieve them and reflect on the learning process itself to improve learning outcomes.

- **1.c.** Use technology to seek feedback that informs and improves their practice and to demonstrate their learning in a variety of ways.

- **3.d.** Build knowledge by actively exploring real-world issues and problems, developing ideas and theories and pursuing answers and solutions.

- **4.a.** Build knowledge by actively exploring real-world issues and problems, developing ideas and theories and pursuing answers and solutions.

- **4.b.** Select and use digital tools to plan and manage a design process that considers design constraints and calculated risks.

- **4.c.** Develop, test and refine prototypes as part of a cyclical design process.

- **4.d.** Exhibit a tolerance for ambiguity, perseverance and the capacity to work with open-ended problems.

- **5.a.** Formulate problem definitions suited for technology-assisted methods such as data analysis, abstract models and algorithmic thinking in exploring and finding solutions.

- **5.c.** Break problems into component parts, extract key information, and develop descriptive models to understand complex systems or facilitate problem-solving.

- **5.d.** Understand how automation works and use algorithmic thinking to develop a sequence of steps to create and test automated solutions.

CHAPTER 10

Robotics in Social Studies

Traditionally, when we think of robots in the K–12 setting, social studies class does not come to mind. We would be hard-pressed to abandon most of our social studies curriculum to begin incorporating computational thinking and robotics into our lessons. However, there are a few simple things we could do to assist our students with making connections to these vital concepts while still aligning with some of the organizing strands (themes) of the National Curriculum Standards for Social Studies, the College, Career, and Civic Life (C3) Framework, and your local social studies standards.

If you recall, Chapter 3 discussed computational thinking and the importance of having students use CT skills prior to programming and coding. Well, social studies is an excellent class to begin doing so, but also bear in mind that when covering these topics, your lessons will have to be interdisciplinary. But then again, real-world learning is typically interdisciplinary and integrative of multiple disciplines in nature. This line of thinking coincides with the definition of social studies by the National Council for the Social Studies (NCSS). Being both the most prominent and largest professional organization for social studies educators, the NCSS defines social studies as:

...the integrated study of the social sciences and humanities to promote civic competence. Within the school program, social studies provides coordinated, systematic study drawing upon such disciplines as anthropology, archaeology, economics, geography, history, law, philosophy, political science, psychology, religion, and sociology, as well as appropriate content from the humanities, mathematics, and natural sciences. The primary purpose of social studies is to help young people make informed and reasoned decisions for the public good as citizens of a culturally diverse, democratic society in an interdependent world. (1992)

Luckily the CSTA K-12 computer science standards provide concepts and subconcepts that assist social studies teachers with creating the alignment to what they already teach, thus making it easier to introduce CT, robotics, and relevant CS material.

Creating Alignment between Social Studies with the CSTA K–12 Computer Science Standards

The CSTA K-12 Computer Science Standards were developed for CS educators, but aspects can also be integrated across disciplines such as social studies. The key to beginning to align the CS standards to any of the social studies frameworks mentioned below (including local frameworks) is to seek out correlations to the five main concepts, subconcepts, and practices they are built on—as described in Figure 3.1 of Chapter 3. And, if you are not sure where to start, we will do that together below.

RESOURCE

K-12 Progression Chart of CSTA Computer Science Standards

Computer Science Teachers Association: *K-12 Progression Chart* (bit.ly/2obimEp)
K-12 progression chart of

Computer Science Teachers Association Computer Science Standards

Unpacking the Thematic Strands for Social Studies

As many social studies educators are aware, in 2010 the NCSS revised the national curriculum social studies standards, which enhanced descriptions of the ten themes along with the accompanying learning expectations. Although this curriculum framework is widely used in schools across many states (and even other nations) as a tool for curriculum development and alignment, the advent of STEM and now CS is rapidly changing the education landscape.

I believe that if schools are truly serious about making CS for all a reality and preparing students for STEM careers, this framework can be leveraged by K-12 social studies teachers to deepen STEM pathways in schools by incorporating essential items for students to know in tandem with their more traditional lessons.

As stated by the NCSS Board of Directors in their Technology Position Statement and Guidelines:

> Technological change has proven one of the few constants of the early 21st century, providing social studies educators with the challenge and opportunity of preparing digital citizens in a global setting. This requires rethinking the type of social studies learning necessary in the 21st century. As the National Academies concluded in the Education for Life and Work report, "the process of deeper learning is essential for the development of transferable 21st century competencies" and "the application of 21st century competencies in turn supports the process of deeper learning, in a recursive, mutually reinforcing cycle. (2013)

Moreover, the NCSS curriculum standards provide a framework for helping schools and educators structure their K-12 social studies programs within ten themes of knowledge about the worldly human experience. As the themes are woven throughout K-12 social studies classes, it is critical to find places where CT, robotics, and aspects of CS can be introduced and incorporated by aligning and correlating to some of the core concepts and practices in the CSTA K-12 Computer Science Standards.

The ten themes are the organizing strands for social studies programs. They are:

1. Culture

2. Time, continuity, and change

3. People, places, and environments

4. Individual development and identity

5. Individuals, groups, and institutions

6. Power, authority, and governance

7. Production, distribution, and consumption

8. Science, technology, and society

9. Global connections

10. Civic ideals and practices

The Themes of Social Studies

National Curriculum Standards for Social Studies: *The Themes of Social Studies* (bit.ly/2GdsPov)

 Thematic Strands for Social Studies

As you can see, there is quite a bit of room for including CT, robotics, and many aspects of computer science into several of these themes. And you will find these in the core CS concepts and subconcepts dealing with computing systems, networks, and the internet (cybersecurity) and impact of computing (culture, social interactions, and safety, laws and ethics).

Additionally, some of the CS practices that can be addressed in social studies can include (but are not limited to) fostering an inclusive computing culture, recognizing and defining computational problems, creating computational artifacts, testing and refining computational artifacts, and communicating about computing. Of course, there are more connections to be made, but this all depends on you, the designer of your lessons.

The College, Career, and Civic Life (C3) Framework

The C3 Framework is another powerful tool that many states use to upgrade their local social studies standards and is also meant for teachers to use for making enhanced instructional shifts for social studies. According to the NCSS, the C3 Framework is driven by the following shared principles about what is regarded as high-quality social studies education:

- Social studies prepares the nation's young people for college, careers, and civic life.

- Inquiry is at the heart of social studies.

- Social studies involves interdisciplinary applications and welcomes integration of the arts and humanities.

- Social studies is composed of deep and enduring understandings, concepts, and skills from the disciplines. Social studies emphasizes skills and practices as preparation for democratic decision-making.

- Social studies education should have direct and explicit connections to the Common Core State Standards for English Language Arts. (NCSS, 2019)

RESOURCE

The College, Career, and Civic Life (C3) Framework

National Council for the Social Studies: *CR Framework* (bit.ly/2XVF3YZ)

Guidance for Enhancing the

Rigor of K-12 Civics, Economics, Geography, and History.

Moreover, the framework utilizes four dimensions on the use of questions for launching student inquiry to guide lessons and classwork and for putting social studies content into authentic, real-world contexts aimed at assisting learners with becoming more active and engaged global citizens. Several items within these dimensions can be strategically aligned to the CS core concepts and subconcepts dealing with networks and the internet (cybersecurity) and impact of computing (culture, social interactions, and safety, laws, and ethics).

Again, some of the CS practices that can be addressed in social studies include (but are not limited to) fostering an inclusive computing culture, recognizing and defining computational problems, creating computational artifacts, testing and refining computational artifacts, and communicating about computing.

Pick the Right Tool for Your Social Studies Classroom

This chapter was trickiest for me to write. This is because social studies education varies from state to state. Although there are common major themes that are relevant to most of the states, some require school divisions to define social studies expectations for students locally while others rely on state adopted standards to inform accountability within instruction and assessment of the discipline.

My aim here was to point out the most obvious and logical connections between the core CS concepts and practices (found in the CSTA standards) that can be connected to both CT and robotics, regardless of what social studies standards the teachers reading this book may use. Moreover, both the National Curriculum Standards for Social Studies: A Framework for Teaching, Learning, and Assessment and the C3 Framework for Social Studies are excellent tools to help guide your work and that is why I dedicated sections to each of them in this chapter. I believe these will be critical for you to use when designing or selecting lessons that include robotics.

Moreover, be mindful about the intended learning and managing of activities to truly remain interdisciplinary while remaining true to the teaching and learning of social studies of your students.

Here are some good places to begin infusing CT as a problem-solving process and robotics as a tool to solve problems:

- Time, continuity and change (students learn about important events and developments)

- People, places, and environments (students learn about relationships between human populations and the physical world, and geography)

- Individual development and identity (students explore careers)

- Individuals, groups, and institutions (students learn how to relate to institutions)

- Production, distribution, and consumption (students learn the production and distribution of goods)

- Science, technology, and society (students learn about careers and the influence of technologies and science on societies)

- Global connections (students learn about the worldwide impact of technology)

The good news is that in many states, social studies teachers have fewer standardized tests to prepare students for and are allowed more autonomy in being creative and authentic (real-world) in their lessons and assessment methods (typically more performance-based). Because social studies are very interdisciplinary, I suggest taking the time to align some of the activities in your units with the CCSS, the ISTE standards, CSTA standards, and the NGSS. Also, do not be afraid to learn about CT, CS, and robotics with your students. For this purpose, I have included some reputable sites for you to check out along with the QR codes.

Social Studies Resources for Robotics Lessons and Curriculum

RESOURCE	DESCRIPTION	ACCESS
Ozobot Lesson Library	Find a variety of social studies-based STEAM lessons as well as other subjects.	(bit.ly/2JSVXTa)
Sphero Edu	Host a large variety of social studies themed lessons and activities.	(bit.ly/2YlQ4qW)
Green Dot Public Schools: *Computational Thinking Curriculum*	CT lessons and projects for social studies.	(bit.ly/2SwoVMA)
Kinder Lab Robotics: *Teacher Materials*	Easy ways to integrate robotics into social studies curriculum.	(bit.ly/30NxqFP)

KinderLab Lesson

KIBO Robotics and Floor Maps— Our Community, Our World and The Historical Journey (or The Travels of Marco KIBO)

KinderLab Robotics
lesson plan for social studies (bit.ly/2OgTtlp)

Overview

KIBO is a robot kit (see figure 10.1) specifically designed for young children (4–7 years old) and floor maps are a perfect complement to KIBO's tangible, hands-on approach to coding. KIBO's journey across the floor map becomes a story told by the children who program it. Through a combination of code and imagination, a floor map becomes a world for children to enter and explore with KIBO. A floor map can represent a physical space, like a student's neighborhood, an animal's natural habitat, or the solar system. It can represent an imaginative space, like the setting of a storybook. And it can even be a concrete representation of an abstract space, such as a palette of all of the class' favorite things, a number line, or a coordinate grid.

Target Grades: K–2

Figure 10.1: KIBO robot.

The Big Idea (Our Community, Our World)

In early childhood, students begin to learn how their lives relate to a larger community and a larger world. A curriculum centered on students' own community is both relevant to their lives and a strong foundation from which they can begin to look outward. A community floor map, such as the one shown in Figure 10.2, is a perfect context for this exploration. KIBO can play the part of familiar vehicles such as school buses and fire trucks as well as the people living in the town.

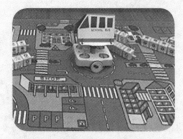

Figure 10.2: Community floor map with KIBO robot in the center.

Duration

90–120 minutes

Materials, Resources, and Teacher Prep

KIBO Robot, floor map, and consumables

Cross-Curricular Learning Goals

- Students reflect on the physical aspects of a community (streets, parks, homes; the natural and built landscapes).

- Students learn more about their own neighborhood.

- Social Studies standards (see standards table)

Vocabulary

Students should know terms such as neighborhoods, towns, cities, states, peoples, places, distant, unfamiliar, geography, maps, and globes, as well as the following:

Code. The set of instructions forming a computer program which is executed by a computer.

Input. Any information or data sent to a computer for processing.

Output. Data generated by a computer.

Algorithm. A set of instructions designed to perform a specific task.

Procedure

1. Organize a walk around the school's immediate neighborhood or just the school environment. Engage the students in discussion about the built and natural features of their neighborhood that they notice.

2. Students work together to create a floor map that represents the school's neighborhood. This does not have to be an accurate map! Students should add to the map elements that are personally meaningful for them, such as their homes, favorite parks or places, or things they noticed on the walk earlier.

3. Student groups decorate their KIBOs to represent an inhabitant of the community: KIBO might be a vehicle such as a school bus or police car, or it might be a person or pet who lives in the neighborhood.

4. Students create programs to represent the life or routine of the character they created. Close the unit with a showcase depicting the life of their neighborhood.

The Big Idea (The Historical Journey)

Learning about events elsewhere in the world and in distant history helps students understand their own lives, but these stories can seem abstract and remote for young children. A floor map can help students visualize the place where a historical event happened; and KIBO can represent a traveler in that place or a participant in the event. This approach brings the concrete, hands-on experience of working with KIBO to social studies and history.

Duration

90–120 minutes

Materials, Resources, and Teacher Prep

KIBO Robot, floor map, and consumables

Cross-Curricular Learning Goals

• Students learn about a historical event and its context.

- Students explore fundamental skills in geography and cartography.

- Students practice putting events in sequence.

- Social Studies standards (see standards table)

Procedure

1. Select an event from history of interest to the class, relevant to the student's families' cultures of origin, or connected to the ongoing curriculum. Through stories, videos, sharing of artifacts, and class discussion, explore the chosen historical event with the students.

2. Students work together to create a floor map that represents the context of the event or culture studied. For example, students might create a large map of the world with their families' countries of origin marked. Or they might represent a historical journey like the 1925 delivery of diphtheria medicine along Alaska's Iditarod Trail.

3. In groups, students decorate their KIBOs as participants in the historical event. KIBO might wear costumes appropriate to the time, become a covered wagon, sailing ship, or dogsled, for example.

4. Students create programs to represent the journey or sequence of events being studied.

5. If you have the Sound Record/Playback Module, students can record facts for their KIBOs to speak, acting as "tour guides" for the map. Even without this Module, students can speak the lines themselves as their KIBO programs run.

6. Close with a showcase where students demonstrate their KIBO historical journeys.

Standards Addressed

National Curriculum Standards for Social Studies

- In the early grades, young learners draw upon immediate personal experiences in their neighborhoods, towns and cities, and states, as well as peoples and places distant and unfamiliar, to explore geographic concepts and skills. They learn to use maps, globes, and other geographic tools.

- Children in early grades learn to locate themselves in time and space. They gain experience with sequencing to establish a sense of order and time, and begin to understand the historical concepts that give meaning to the events that they study.

CSTA K-12 Computer Science Standards

- **1A-AP-08:** Model daily processes by creating and following algorithms (sets of step-by-step instructions) to complete tasks.

- **1A-AP-10:** Develop programs with sequences and simple loops, to express ideas or address a problem.

- **1A-AP-11:** Decompose (break down) the steps needed to solve a problem into a precise sequence of instructions.

ISTE Standards for Students

- **1.a.** Articulate and set personal learning goals, develop strategies leveraging technology to achieve them and reflect on the learning process itself to improve learning outcomes.

- **1.c.** Use technology to seek feedback that informs and improves their practice and to demonstrate their learning in a variety of ways.

- **3.d.** Build knowledge by actively exploring real-world issues and problems, developing ideas and theories and pursuing answers and solutions.

- **4.a.** Build knowledge by actively exploring real-world issues and problems, developing ideas and theories and pursuing answers and solutions.

- **4.c.** Develop, test and refine prototypes as part of a cyclical design process.

- **4.d.** Exhibit a tolerance for ambiguity, perseverance and the capacity to work with open-ended problems.

- **5.a.** Formulate problem definitions suited for technology-assisted methods such as data analysis, abstract models and algorithmic thinking in exploring and finding solutions.

- **5.c.** Break problems into component parts, extract key information, and develop descriptive models to understand complex systems or facilitate problem-solving.

- **5.d.** Understand how automation works and use algorithmic thinking to develop a sequence of steps to create and test automated solutions.

Strategies and Approaches for Teaching Robotics and Computational Thinking

This final section provides teachers the importance of using what we know from the learning sciences to begin incorporating educational robotics (ER), computational thinking (CT), and aspects of computer science (CS) into our classroom lessons and projects. Constructivism as a paradigm for teaching and learning is explained along with examples of strategies teachers can employ with ER and CT for constructivist learning (including PBL). The author provides an original exemplar with actionable steps for embedding ER, CT, and programming in PBL in tandem with curricular resources. The final chapter also provides practical tips for establishing an afterschool club and how to get started with competitive robotics.

The chapters in this section explore:

- **Constructivist teaching and learning**
- **Evidence-based strategies**
- **Project Based Learning (PBL)**
- **Author example of embedding CT, robotics, and programming in PBL**
- **Robotics outside of school**

Robotics, Constructivist Learning, and Infusing the Learning Sciences

In Chapter 5 we learned that elements of constructivism inform the theory for many (if not most) of the documented learning activities with educational robotics (ER). Furthermore, constructivist teaching and learning also provides the theoretical framework for many of the popular instructional strategies, instructional planning approaches, and scripted CS and robotics curriculum in today's schools.

CS and robotics teachers should understand why and how such practices help students learn and find ways of leveling up their own instructional design (ID) and teaching practices for enhancing the experience of all learners.

Before beginning my doctoral journey, I always knew that both my approach to ID and teaching was laden with constructivist elements—as I believe that learners learn best by doing and by reflecting for metacognition. However, I was unaware of the learning theories that made up constructivism or how they informed the theoretical frameworks in many of the instructional planning methods and active learning strategies I used in my work.

In the last couple of years, I have begun to understand the learning theories that anchor both ID and several of the prominent research studies that affected the classrooms of both myself and the teachers I have worked with over the years. Unfortunately, either no one told us what they were, or we were oblivious when they did.

I came to know that my previous understanding was only based on years of practice. And although I eventually became a good lesson planner and facilitator (by using evidence-based strategies and educational protocols), I realized that I could not explain to others why my teaching strategies were sound. I just knew that they worked.

Using Constructivism to Teach CS

For teachers wishing to understand how constructivism informs CS curriculum and most of the lessons in this book, I believe it is important to understand the following three items:

1. How constructivism develops

2. How to develop awareness of how constructivism relates to student learning

3. How to develop your identity for constructivist teaching

Understand how constructivism develops.

Know that constructivism is a paradigm for teaching and learning and is an amalgamation of the behavioral and cognitive learning theories and that it shows up in other theories as well (general systems theory and communications theory, among others). Moreover, mapping or illustrating something this complex is not easy because it seems to be always evolving, mainly due to the diverse ways that technology is used to augment instruction.

This is clearly depicted in the concept map by author Michael Lacoursiere shown in Figure 11.1. As concept maps are used for depicting the relationships between concepts, this map makes it easy to see that constructivism is not linear (lacks structure) but can be accessed through tested ID models and frameworks that are more linear and systematic (Understanding by Design (UbD), Workshop Model, High Quality Project Based Learning (HQPBL), among others) and possess constructivist elements.

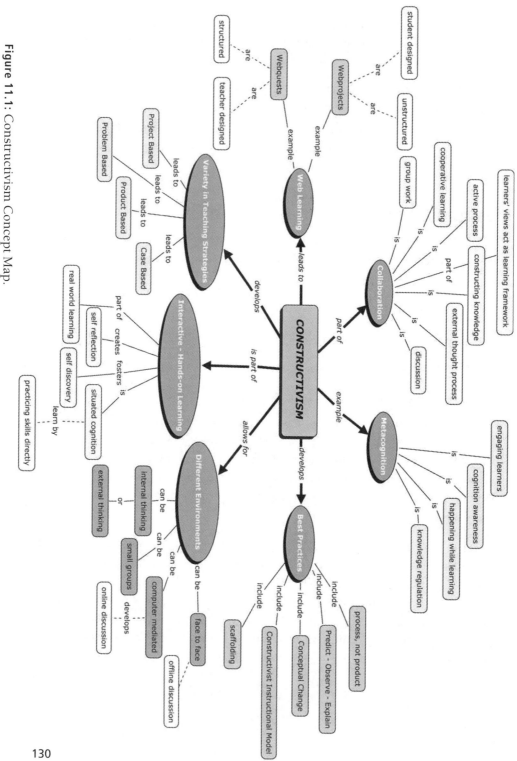

Figure 11.1: Constructivism Concept Map.
Source: Michael Lacoursiere

Develop awareness of how constructivism relates to student learning.

As a paradigm for teaching and learning, constructivism says that people construct their own understanding and knowledge of the world through experiencing things and reflecting on those experiences. In the classroom, the goals of constructivism are problem-solving, higher-order thinking skills, and collaboration.

Guiding student learning to achieve these goals can be done using essential, guiding, and driving questions. Making our questions engaging, open-ended, and aligned with student learning goals launches student inquiry and provides us more in-depth insight into the academic needs of our learners.

Students who lack either declarative or procedural knowledge may get stuck in problem-solving when attempting to answer the guiding or driving question. When they do not know specific facts or steps to solve a problem, they will get stuck, need help, and many will give up. To prevent this, I find activities that will inform me of how to accurately serve my students better than having them simply build robots or code using tutorials or step-by-step instructions. Moreover, teachers who rely on constructivist approaches will have to glean from what occurs in the classroom to both determine and maximize their time with students. Teachers can considerably improve their practices by:

- Using instructional approaches and activities that cause students to learn experientially (i.e., problem-based learning, project based learning, service learning, simulations, and role-playing).

- Using engaging student-centered instructional design and teaching practices to help students construct learning in meaningful ways. Some examples of this are backward design planning and using protocols such as Best Ever, Charette, and the Question Formulation Technique.

- Helping students connect previous knowledge to new knowledge through effective scaffolded instruction and gradually reducing the scaffolds as students become more independent and can problem solve more on their own.

- Having students interact with professionals for more authentic and real-world work that allows them to take more active roles in both what they create and whom they create for (i.e., addressing problems, challenges, or issues in the community).

- Engaging students by making them take an active role in their learning as they have more voice and choice over how they transfer learning (examples of transfer may include public service announcements, mock TED talks, writing blogs, and presentations).

Develop your identity for constructivist teaching.

On a personal note, I was not engaged in significant constructivist active learning opportunities by many of my teachers before embarking on my PBL journey with PBLWorks (Buck Institute for Education). My reason for learning PBL was because several colleagues told me that it would be a very practical approach to teaching STEM and CS-related content.

It has taken me many years to seek out the right professional development to develop my identity as a constructivist teacher and gain the expertise to be able to engage learners to be active participants in their own learning. And although leveling up my practice through PBL and other constructivist practice has been ongoing, it has provided me roadmaps to follow rather than winging it in my classroom.

For teachers who are beginning or wanting to enhance their constructivist teaching practices, they should realize it is a process that will not occur quickly—and should be aware of the following:

- One needs to be a very skilled practitioner and this will take both practice and time.

- It is easier to use instructional models and frameworks that have specific protocols for engaging students actively (which is why I chose PBL)

- It is difficult to learn and do by yourself. Teachers and students often need modeling, coaching, and scaffolding.

- Constructivism is not an exclusive practice for every student or lesson.

- Learners often assess themselves, which could cause them to fall behind if they do not understand how to use assessment tools such as rubrics and checklists.

- Teachers have much planning to do prior to and after meeting with their learners.

- Teachers should frequently participate in book studies with colleagues.

- Consider becoming active learning partners with students, meaning you *do not* have to know everything. This practice is useful when having to earn learners' trust, teach new material, or in disciplines such as computer science or engineering where many teachers are teaching topics without much expertise or prior exposure to the content they are teaching.

Although a lot of this can initially seem overwhelming, I would like you to consider learning to tackle these items by adopting PBL in your classroom. PBL is a teaching strategy that encompasses much of what is discussed in this chapter regarding constructivist teaching and can also be implemented using evidence-based strategies. For this purpose, the next chapter is dedicated to helping readers understand how to use PBL within the context of robotics and computational thinking.

CHAPTER 12

Project Based Learning (PBL) and Robotics

The recent push in education reform to make schoolwork more relevant has alerted most education stakeholders to the fact that STEM and other forms of interdisciplinary and experiential learning is a way to better engage students and can also be leveraged to help create a more viable workforce. PBL is rapidly becoming the go-to instructional approach for school redesign throughout the United States and in other parts of the world. Among the countries adopting PBL are Finland, Spain, Australia, and China.

The PBL strategy facilitates teaching and learning with educational robotics (ER) and computational thinking when the context of projects is authentic and focuses on building foundations in the principles discussed throughout this book. I myself have taught CT and robotics to my students (as well as other branches of CS) and before I provide examples from my classroom, let's get a better understanding of PBL.

Why Project Based Learning (PBL) and What Is It?

According to PBLWorks (2019), "Project Based Learning (PBL) prepares students for academic, personal, and career success, and readies young people to rise to the challenges of their lives and the world they will inherit." For teachers wishing to engage their students in CT and robotics, PBL can really bring the content to life in ways that solely following scripted curriculum and tutorials step-by-step cannot.

Please do not misinterpret my previous statement and assume that we just contradicted the use of scripted curriculum as highlighted and discussed in part two of this book. Scripted curriculum definitely has its place in the classroom because it assists teachers who are still learning new content by providing activities that are readily available to be implemented with students. Moreover, one of my goals with that section of this book is to honor the previous and amazing work of teaching and learning with robotics that others in education have done to pave the way for me and millions of educators worldwide.

The goal of this section is to explain how teachers can leverage ER and CT activities found in scripted curriculum in the context of a teacher-developed PBL unit aimed to serve the personal needs of the students they teach in their classrooms. This can be done as teachers develop a deeper understanding of teaching with ER and CT in tandem with incorporating the elements found in reputable PBL models and frameworks to their lessons.

Frameworks and Model of Excellence

There are several models and frameworks for PBL but for our purposes, I will briefly elaborate on two that are reputable, researched based, and highly accessible for any teacher or school to implement.

High Quality Project Based Learning (HQPBL) Framework

The High Quality Project Based Learning (HQPBL) Framework was established in 2018 and is a consensus of both research and the accumulated practice of PBL leaders throughout the world. This work was sponsored by the Buck Institute for Education (now PBLWorks) and was supported by the Project Management Institute Educational Foundation (PMIEF) and the William and Flora Hewlett Foundation. In addition, some of the partners include Google, High Tech High, EL Education, Southern Regional Education Board, and ISTE.

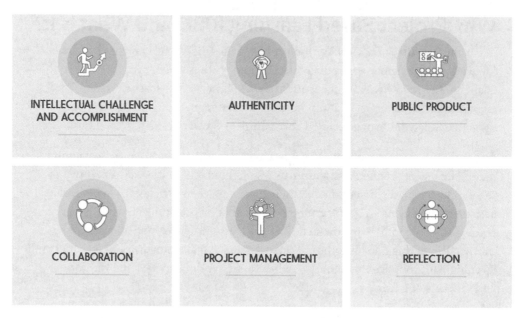

Figure 12.1: High Quality Project Based Learning Framework. Source: hqpbl.org

High Quality Project Based Learning Framework

HQPBL Framework

(bit.ly/2ONiFSd)

 Downloadblle frameworkforhigh quality project based learning.

The HQPBL framework describes six minimal criteria (see Figure 12.1). Each must be present in some form in a project for it to be deemed as "high quality" PBL.

The framework is backed by research that indicates that students who have high quality experiences in PBL demonstrate deeper learning outcomes. In the downloadable framework, each of the six criteria are explained in detail along with indicators of high quality. Furthermore, the framework outlines PBL from the perspective of students and is designed to provide all educators a shared basis for designing and implementing projects that are of high quality.

Gold Standard Project Based Learning (GSPBL)

Since 1999, PBLWorks (formally known as Buck Institute for Education) has focused exclusively on PBL and is a recognized world leader for PBL resources such as research, professional development, publications, project exemplars, planning forms, rubrics, and methodology for PBL—which is aptly titled Gold Standard Project Based Learning (GSPBL).

GSPBL is a research-based model built on two frameworks: the Essential Project Design Elements and the Project Based Teaching Practices (See Figure 12.2). I like to call them the *what* and the *how*: what (project design elements) should go into a gold standard PBL unit and how (project based teaching practices) it should be taught.

For the past six years, I have had the privilege of being a national faculty member of PBLWorks. During this time, I have received extensive training in GSPBL, educational protocols, restorative practices, equity centered teaching, and curriculum development aimed at improving the PBL practices of teachers, myself included. In any given year, I coach roughly between 300-500 educators and guide them through the development of GSPBL units. I often return to their schools and have seen firsthand the results and effects of GSPBL on both teachers and students. It is in these workshops where I have developed a keen sense for knowing what teachers need and then providing them the right tailored assistance with PBL.

When working in my role as a national faculty member, I work with entire K-16 schools and faculties. In my own classroom and workshops I apply GSPBL in the context of CS, CT, STEM, and of course robotics. This practice has amplified the learning of my students and I highly recommend that you too begin to use PBL correctly in your own practice. If a PBLWorks workshop is not available in your district, seek out a PBL institute close to your area. You will not regret doing so.

I will use the remaining portion of this chapter to provide examples from my own classroom of how I use PBL to teach students CT and robotics. I will also provide access to a PBL unit I developed. Use it to level up your own teaching of the content found in this book.

Resources for PBL Design and Practice

PBLWorks: *Gold Standard PBL— Essential Project Design Elements* (bit.ly/2yQSnUt)

This blogpost shares design elements to consider when creating gold standard PBL.

PBLWorks: *Gold Standard PBL— Project Based Teaching Practices* (bit.ly/2KtCLwK)

This blogpost shares best practices for teaching gold standard PBL.

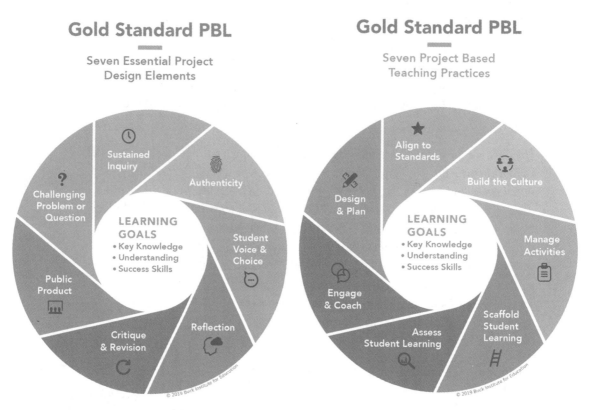

Figure 12.2: Gold Standard Project Based Learning Model. Source: PBLWorks

The Computational Thinkers Project

Aspects of the following Computational Thinkers Project have previously been covered in how-to blogs published by ISTE and PBLWorks. I also developed the project in the PBLWorks project planner and used GSPBL in both my planning and delivery methods. I share these resources in the QR codes that follow, but first, I explain the premise of the project and how CT, programming robots, and game-based coding were taught to students in five steps. I chose to focus on these two aspects of the project because, as previously noted, these are the foundational skills needed for more complex work with programming robots.

Project Summary

In the Computational Thinkers Project, students learn to apply the elements of computational thinking as a problem-solving skill to both unplugged and coding scenarios. As CT is understandable to both machines and humans, students will learn to draw on familiar concepts that connect their previous learning to foundational CS practices that involve designing solutions that leverage the power of computing by programming robots and creating an original game design using coding and programming skills. Throughout the project, students will interact with CS experts, work in teams, and assume the roles of either software engineers, software developers, or programmers. The students will also teach their new CT and CS to younger peers and present their work publicly to parents, school administrators, and others in the community.

The driving question for the project was, "How can we as computational thinkers design a children's game that teaches younger peers foundational coding skills and the use of electronic circuits?"

My goal was to have students learn to apply the elements of CT as a problem-solving skill to both unplugged and plugged scenarios before doing so through coding to fully answer the driving question.

CT, which is standard five of the ISTE Standards for Students, can be applied by both machines and humans. I therefore purposefully coached students using the evidence-based strategies of learning targets and the jigsaw strategy to help them create and present computational artifacts.

As I coached students, they were able to draw on familiar concepts and connect CT to foundational computer science practices that involve designing solutions that leverage the power of computing, at the same time improving their literacy and collaboration skills.

Step 1: The Mini-Lesson

To introduce students to CT, the learning targets, the jigsaw strategy, and the final product they were responsible for, I conducted a mini-lesson. Mini-lessons are excellent for sparking interest in topics, generating questions, and introducing strategies to learners. I strategically leveraged their power in the following ways.

STUDENT INQUIRY

I showed students an artifact depicting the CT elements, which included the graphic shown in Figure 12.3, for generating their own questions. Their questions were then curated in the form of a "need-to-know" list. Both the artifact and the list were used to launch student inquiry and point them in the direction of both CT and coding, which I used to guide future lessons within the unit of study.

LEARNING TARGETS

To scaffold their thinking, I gave students learning targets so they understood the intended learning and expectations. I answered clarifying questions and helped them define new vocabulary (i.e., CT, computational artifact, flowchart, and role play) in the learning targets. The learning targets for the lesson were:

- I can investigate and understand one of the four computational thinking elements.

- I can apply one or more of the four computational thinking elements through both roleplay and a computational artifact.

- I can develop a step-by-step algorithm for a personal task of my choosing using a flowchart (painting my nails, walking my dog, etc.).

I then partnered students in groups of three or four in preparation for the jigsaw strategy.

Step 2: The Jigsaw Strategy

For the purpose of having the students learn CT in tandem with problem-solving, using higher-order thinking skills, and collaborating with peers, I used the jigsaw strategy. Developed by Dr. Elliot Aronson and his students at the universities of California and Texas, the jigsaw is a cooperative learning strategy where students in a group divvy up the learning by each researching one aspect and teaching it to the others.

When executed effectively, there is evidence that the jigsaw strategy also aids learners with mastering topics, improving literacy skills, spurring motivation, and increasing enjoyment of the learning experience. In fact, an updated version of John Hattie's list of influences on student learning places the jigsaw strategy among the top ten ways students learn, with an effect size of 1.20–which is three times more

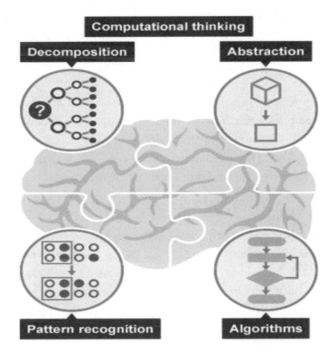

Figure 12.3: Computational Thinking Elements. Source: BBC

effective and quite a leap from the average effect size (.40) of the other strategies found in Hattie's database.

To implement the strategy, I had the students become experts on one of the four CT elements (decomposition, abstraction, pattern recognition, and algorithm design) by following this process:

LEARNING

In homogeneous expert groups, the students read and analyzed text (using annotating text strategies) about their element in the ISTE article "How to develop computational thinkers." To help them visualize what they read, some also created concept maps to share and connect their new understandings.

Using a rubric, the expert teams then created a synthesis in the form of a computational artifact. Here the students were provided voice and choice on how they would transfer learning using edtech tools such as Canva, videos, podcasts, and Google Slides.

For their computational artifacts, they created definitions for their CT element and cited personal relevance to it by correlating it to an everyday familiar task or activity (i.e., making a sandwich, tying a shoelace, brushing teeth, etc.). Each team also created original graphics to represent their element.

Finally, the students read the blogpost "Guide to Flowchart Symbols, from Basic to Advanced" by Samie Kaufman (bit.ly/33nQITl) and learned about the basics of making flowcharts and the universal flowchart symbols of process, input/output, decision, start/end, and arrows. Some students created a flowchart of the steps they took during their roleplay and others chose to diagram new problems.

SHARING

The expert teams returned to a heterogeneous group setting and presented and discussed their learning in a mini-presentation format. No more than six minutes was allotted for each group but Q&A did run over a bit. The students displayed their computational artifacts in a professional way as they discussed their CT element and the logic in their flowchart algorithm. However, they really came alive during their roleplays. We witnessed fun, excitement, and transfer of learning that I was extremely proud of.

DEEPENING THE LEARNING

In this final step of jigsaw strategy, the students returned to their expert groups and discussed how their CT element fit along with the other elements their classmates presented within the broader context of computational thinking as both a problem-solving and higher-order thinking skill.

They also revisited the ISTE article we presented them in the first step of the jigsaw strategy to base their discussions in the broader context of the entire text. My purpose here was to help them deepen their understanding of both the text and the importance of CT as a series of foundational skills needed for future CS learning. At this time, I also introduced a collaboration rubric and had them discuss three things they did right and three things to improve for the next time by reviewing the indicators together.

Step 3: Allow for Play with Edtech—Robotics with the Sphero BOLT

To keep my students fully engaged throughout the length of the project, I made time for play each time we met by incorporating edtech that allowed them to implement their new CT skills and that would help scaffold future coding lessons.

For this purpose, I introduced them to the Sphero BOLT, an app-enabled robot that through play (in our class context), helped lay the foundation for CS and coding with a programmable LED (light-emitting diode) matrix. Through guided play, my students used the BOLT to explore both its coding and gaming capabilities by learning about infrared communication, sensors, acceleration, direction, tracking speed, and aiming the robot by using it as a compass.

Note to teachers: Not all students initially learned all the concepts, but through guided practice and a selection of activities, I have found playtime with edtech to be a critical component for fostering the deepening of learning and fun in my classroom. When allowing for play, be sure that the edtech you choose connects to your daily lesson and the final product that the students are working on.

Step 4: Student Reflection

A John Dewey quote that I shared with my students is, "We do not learn from experience. We learn from reflecting on experience." Incorporating reflection into my work with them is something that I did at various stages. I found the practice helped the students make critical connections, learn from failure, and deepen their understanding of CT.

In this particular lesson, students reflected by writing in journals. I then followed up with them in either whole-group discussions or individual consultations. Among the reflections I asked students to make were:

- Why are computational thinking concepts and practices important for me to learn and use?

- How can I correlate computational thinking to what I already know?

- How are computational thinking skills used to program robots such as the Sphero BOLT?

- How can I introduce the concept of computational thinking to others (i.e., younger peers) in a presentation?

Student responses included:

- I can use CT as a problem-solving strategy in both familiar and unfamiliar situations that I encounter in my life.

- I can use algorithm design strategies to learn the steps to solving problems with math formulas and the code when programming a robot.

- I can create a YouTube video or podcast to help teach my peers about the CT elements.

By helping students connect their new learning to specific situations in and out of school and understand how they can use CT to help others, I gained more know-how for developing design thinkers who are also global citizens (as emphasized in the ISTE Standards for Students).

Step 5: Using littleBits to Teach Electronics and Coding

Now that my students were computational thinking enabled, it was time to have them work on their game designs with littleBits. LittleBits makes the use of electronics, game-based coding, and also the preparatory and exploratory skillsets needed for design/invention highly accessible for any teacher or student.

For this particular project, the littleBits were a perfect complement to the Sphero BOLT (the edtech I used in step 3) because it helped my students develop further capacity for understanding core concepts and practices in robotics and CS. Another plus is that the similar LED matrix, motors, sensors, and coding/programming skills that are used in the Sphero BOLT (and other robotics tools) are also applied in littleBits.

Not new to the process, my students italicized new vocabulary (topics) in the driving question and underlined the items they already knew. My goal was to have them focus on new learning and how it connects to any previous knowledge for the game design.

Sample: "How can we as *computational thinkers* design a children's game that teaches younger peers <u>foundational coding skills</u> and the use of electronic circuits?"

I gave students a short list of game design ideas to choose from, and some of them decided to learn and remix one of the built-in Code Kit inventions. Others created an original invention.

Some of the learning targets (LTs) I wanted students to understand were:

- I can decompose each step of the coding process into minute details so that I can explain to others.

- I can recognize patterns (similarities or common differences) that will help me make predictions about which bits (input, output, power, etc.) are appropriate for my game design.

- I can abstract any unnecessary information while coding my program.

- I can develop a step-by-step algorithm for a personal task of my choosing (painting my nails, walking my dog, etc.).

- I can develop step-by-step algorithms of code for the game program.

- I can define and apply loops in the game program.

- I can use variables to store data to be referenced for the game program.

- I can define and apply conditional logic in the game program.

- I can apply the remix step in the littleBits Invention Cycle to create new code for my game.

Note to teachers: The LTs used for this work were the rewriting (unpacking) of some indicators listed for the CT strand in the ISTE Standards for Students, the littleBits Code Kit lesson plans, and the CSTA standards.

LTs should be written in student-friendly language and are an excellent strategy for helping students focus learning, build vocabulary, and request specific feedback. I highly recommend knowing the do's and don'ts when designing learning targets for students. For this purpose, I highly recommend a helpful rubric and videos by EL Education to get started (eleducation.org/resources/chapter-1-learning-targets).

The Game Design

To transfer their new CT skills and help others, the students created inventions by designing a model that would help younger children understand the importance of electronic circuits, coding, and technologies encountered in everyday life while enjoying a game.

Using the littleBits Code Kit, they built the foundation of their games based on instructions and tinkered before settling on an original design. And through visual programming, they were able to recognize patterns, functions, and purpose of both the hardware and code.

Upon mastering the new technology and various coding principles (apply loops, use variables to store data to be referenced, and conditional logic), the students developed step-by-step solution algorithms that they coded using Google Blockly-based code. For example, some used code to control a timer, message, and image display on the LED matrix of their game design. Before deciding on a final automated solution, they also tested and redid their algorithmic designs several times to make it to their liking.

Note to teachers: During work time, it's essential for you to facilitate learning. When working with groups of students, it's important to be well versed in the use of the Code Kit (or whatever technology you are using in your lessons/projects) and its app. Use the app to help you conduct mini-lessons and scaffolds of the coding concepts your learners need most (either individually or in groups). To achieve this effectively I like to use the workshop model for my station rotations and they are conducted as follows:

- Programming with the teacher

- Programming with a partner (pair programming)

- Individually building foundational coding skills using Code Kit app tutorials

Don't forget to engage students in a design process. My students used the littleBits invention cycle and the invention log checklist on page 16 of the code kit invention log to assess their work. I also highly recommend having the debugging checklist and the feedback chart. Also, use feedback protocols and the LTs to help students request and receive feedback for improving their work. These resources can be accessed using the QR code for the littleBits Code Kit.

How to Use the Workshop Model for Coding

When teaching students to write code for programming robots (or other devices), it is unlikely that all of them will be coding at the same level. Therefore it is important to employ sound teaching strategies for making learning the material accessible to all of them.

For this purpose, I like to draw inspiration from the Workshop Model (WM) developed by Carmen Farina and Lucy Calkins (for enhancing literacy). The WM structure allows teachers to organize and monitor learning while helping students become more responsible for their own mastery as they build competence for coding and programming. Engaging them in this structure also leads to increased confidence and willingness to extend their presumed capabilities for the multilayered skills.

In my adaptation of the WM as briefly mentioned above in step 5, I still conduct my mini-lessons but allow groups of students to create programs and increase their coding skills with appropriate activities for their varied levels. Using the Code Kit app, teachers can facilitate learning for learners new to coding by having them participate in the following station rotations within the WM structure.

1. **Coding with the teacher (write your first program):** In coding there is a tradition for creating our first program and how software developers test a system they are using for the first time—it's called "Hello World." For learners that are very new, having me model and coach by their side gives them the confidence that they too can code their first program.

2. **Pair programming (code with a partner):** Pair programming (PP) is a strategy used in the workplace by software developers and students in computer science classes for learning collaboratively and completing big and complex projects. When both partners are newbies, the PP strategy can have potential pitfalls in the learning. Therefore, be sure to have students use rubrics and make time for frequent teacher check-ins and student reflection.

3. **Learn the core concepts using personalized tutorials:** As students gain more confidence with both the core concepts and edtech—I allow them to build further mastery independently by using tutorials that address very specific coding skills (loops, functions, etc.). Again, have them use rubrics and provide frequent check-ins.

Lastly, coding and programming are multilayered skills that require time, patience, effective use of edtech, and sound strategies for achieving mastery. Moreover, creating a programmer can take years and cannot happen in one class, semester, or lesson. Therefore, focus your teaching and learning on the basics, building student capacity for the more complex tasks and getting them where they need to be—which is the rigor level that is appropriate for their current understanding and grade level.

Resources for Computational Thinkers Project

Sphero Education: *Sphero Bolt* (bit.ly/2q0PBLh)

Information abnd curriculum for the Sphero BOLT app-enabled robot.

LittleBits Education: *Code Kit Curriculum* (bit.ly/2MkxVl2)

Teacher lesson plans and student handouts for the LittleBits Code Kit.

Lifelong Learning Defined: *The Computational Thinkers Project*

Planner (bit.ly/ CT_Thinkers_Project_Planner) Project planner and other documents.

Robotics Outside of School

Due to current trends in education reform such as "computer science for all" and the desire for many teachers to make teaching and learning relevant with real-world skills in their classrooms, the previous section of this book focused on incorporating robotics and computational thinking into lessons using standards-based skills. However, many schools still want to offer additional learning opportunities with robotics as part of robust outside of school (OST) programs.

But if you are still on the fence and not sure if afterschool is your best route, use the pro tips provided in this chapter for motivation and helping you to either get started or enhance an existing OST program.

Getting Started

Are you interested in starting an afterschool robotics club at your school and need some reasons to start? Remember that afterschool allows for learning in a low-stakes environment without the pressure of grades and testing, which helps us create a safe space for both teachers and students to learn from trial and error while building competence and confidence for solving problems with robotics.

Afterschool is the ideal learning environment for starting in schools with an emphasis on high-stakes assessment. Angst can be easily conquered with the following steps:

Step 1: Use the first section of this book to learn what robotics is and why it is useful in the real world. Then use chapters 4-5 to build your understanding of computational thinking and the basics for both building and programming robots. Although the example used in chapter 5 is for VEX, the principles will apply to most educational robotics (ER) tools. Chapters 6-10 provide QR codes to various ER tools and curriculum for getting started.

Step 2: Depending on the content you teach during the instructional day, use the corresponding chapter in section two (chapters 6-10) for making the appropriate connections to your teaching context.

Step 3: Use the detailed steps described in chapter 2 (see listed steps below) to simplify preparing for an afterschool club and/or competitive robotics.

1. Garner the support of your school administration.

2. Create a written plan of how robotics will meet the academic needs of students.

3. Poll students to gauge their buy-in.

4. Create a list of needed items and a budget.

5. Create a realistic timeline.

6. Find teacher and parent helpers.

7. Determine storage and meeting location.

8. Keep communication open.

9. Use social media.

10. Improve your own learning gaps.

Have a Vision for Your Intended Outcomes

Once you have support for your afterschool club, it is important to determine your intended outcomes, tools, curriculum, and pathway(s) for teaching and learning with ER. Typically, a good club combines the interest of the teacher with activities that will attract a diverse pool of students. Following are some helpful categories to consider.

Build STEM awareness with ER.

Here I recommend using one of the chapters from section two (any from 6–10) for helping you pick the right tool and lesson(s) for working with students. Here I emphasize explicitly having students use computational thinking and the engineering design process within the context of long-term projects. If you have students for an entire semester (or two quarters), I recommend at least two or three good projects within that time frame. Also, be sure to celebrate the learning by inviting stakeholders to see your students present their projects.

Apply math and science skills with ER.

This theme will always be a winner with students, parents, and administrators and is extremely helpful for providing students a real-world context to both math and science work. Math teachers should use chapter 8 and science teachers chapter 9 for a precise list of the right ER tools and standards-based activities aligned to the CCSS and the NGSS. Here teachers can focus more on problem-based learning instead of doing elaborate projects. However, do let your kids engage in some ER play in tandem with your lessons. For example, if I hold students for two hours after school, I typically allow them 30 minutes to explore and play toward the end of OST.

Explore competitive robotics.

Although this option may seem daunting to newbies, it really doesn't have to be. Your best bet is to center your club around annual regional and or state competitions. Doing so provides focus and purpose to your weekly meetings and activities. However, if it is your first go around, do not go at it alone until you learn the ropes. Find a mentor(s) and make sure that they have already managed or are managing a successful robotics club, preferably in your local area. That will enable them to provide you with accurate information regarding the right competitive events for you and your students.

Consider the costs.

Competitive robotics will require you to invest in expensive kits and competition event fees—which often include travel (i.e., transportation, hotels, and food). Make sure to have these items secured or a fundraising plan if needed. If you are not sure where to start, the fundraising toolkit by FIRST Robotics is helpful (firstinspires. org/resource-library/fundraising-toolkit).

Consider robotics competitions.

I highly recommend enrolling in competitive events that are popular within your region and state. This will cut back on travel time and give you access to a wider professional learning network of others working toward similar goals. Here is a list of some of the most popular robotics events for you to consider. Most are probably within your network reach:

- **Boosting Engineering, Science & Technology (BEST) Robotics Competitions (bestrobotics.org/site)**
- **FIRST LEGO League (firstinspires.org/robotics/fll)**
- **FIRST Tech Challenge (firstinspires.org/robotics/ftc)**
- **VEX Robotics Competitions (vexrobotics.com/competition)**
- **Wonder League Robotics (makewonder.com/classroom/robotics-competition)**
- **Zero Robotics Tournament (zerorobotics.mit.edu/tournaments)**

Consider time.

If this is your first time preparing students for competitive events, you will be learning through failure and repetition. Although this takes time, repetition will help your team build expertise. With that said, please do not make winning the primary goal for your students. Instead, focus on learning, improving, refining robot designs/programs, and, most importantly, having FUN! Lastly, learning alongside your students will inspire and motivate them to learn more.

Conclusion

Thank you, reader, for taking the time to make this journey with me by investing in the time to read and implement the advice and lessons in this book. No doubt, learning and teaching how to build and program high-level robotics is not easy and is a time-consuming process. It has also become a matter of educational equity and a must-have in all schools if we are serious about equipping all students (in particular those furthest from opportunity) with the right career skills required for the 21st century and beyond.

Because learning robotics is part of the endeavor needed for helping to develop students who will become great engineers and computer scientists, I urge our school leaders to take the advice put forward in this book for taking measured steps toward the sustainable development of teachers in their schools. We do not have the luxury of passing the buck and keeping our fingers crossed, hoping that students will learn robotics and programming in college. We need to start in K–12 as an ongoing, lifelong process that is reinforced in every discipline by having every student learn to think computationally for practical problem-solving.

A.P.J. Abdul Kalam once said, "Great teachers emanate out of knowledge, passion, and compassion." Moreover, I believe that great students need great teachers who are willing to expand their knowledge base for no other reason than it's what kids everywhere need. Doing so is not only an investment in our teachers, students, workforce, and economy, but also an investment in our country (wherever that may be) and our global community at large.

With gratitude,
Jorge

Resources

If you're interested in professional development and more information for the items discussed in this book, I'd recommend you look into the following resources.

Professional Development in Pedagogy

- **ISTEU: Online Courses (iste.org/learn/iste-u)** ISTE U is a virtual hub of best-in-class courses to help all educators build and explore digital age competencies. By working with leading educators and education organizations, ISTE brings you impactful, engaging courses that put pedagogy first and provide incredible learning from the moment you get started!

- **Lifelong Learning Defined Workshops (lifelonglearningdefined.com/services)** Lifelong Learning Defined (LLD) strives to provide all educators practical steps to take in learning, planning, and applying computational thinking (CT) computer science (CS) and STEM related concepts and practices into instruction with all students. LLD also provides a system(s) for measuring educator progress when participating in professional development and or working with students in CS and STEM related content. For educators and schools, LLD also provides authentic solutions, best practices, and resources for helping them master and weave CT, CS, STEM concepts, and practices into both classrooms and schoolwide instructional models.

- **Teach Better Speakers Network (teachbetter.com/speakersnetwork)** The Teach Better Speakers Network is dedicated to supporting the entire school ecosystem. Covering a variety of educational topics and services, each speaker aims to support educators in the field toward creating and maintaining a progressive, student-focused classroom.

- **PBLWorks: PBL 101 Workshop (pblworks.org/services)** PBLWorks builds the capacity of educators to design and facilitate high quality Project Based Learning (PBL). In addition, PBLWorks leads the nation in research, publications, project exemplars, planning forms, rubrics, and Gold Standard Project Based Learning.

Professional Development in CS and STEM

Learning to teach effectively is critical for any subject we teach. However, increasing our content knowledge in that subject is equally imperative. For this reason, I highly recommend the right professional organizations and professional learning networks (PLNs) for keeping abreast of the latest concepts, practices, trends, and use of edtech for computer science and STEM.

Join the Computer Science Teachers Association (CSTA) (csteachers.org). The CSTA understands that teaching computer science can be hard; however, you're not in this alone. As a CSTA member, you are a part of a community that:

- Is led by K–12 computer science teachers, and puts teacher needs at the forefront

- Shares the latest best practices in K–12 computer science education

- Creates local communities across the U.S. and Canada that make sure every computer science teacher has a home

- Builds the largest teacher-led computer science professional development event in the world each year

- Provides access to exclusive discounts on courses and tools that will take your teaching practice to the next level

Join the ISTE Computer Science Network (bit.ly/35sRjUx). The ISTE Computer Science Network is dedicated to the promotion of computational thinking and computer science education. The network promotes and provides ideas, resources and events for integrating computational thinking and computer science into every school and classroom to create equitable access for all students.

Join the ISTE STEM Network (bit.ly/2QPRCne). The STEM Network's purpose is to connect science, technology, engineering and math educators to discuss, explore and share best practices and research in STEM teaching and student learning through the use of technology.

Join the International Technology and Engineering Educators Association (iteea.
org/Community/Membership.aspx). The International Technology and Engineering Educators Association (ITEEA) is an excellent professional organization
for technology and engineering educators. The mission of the organization is to
promote technological literacy for all by supporting the teaching practices of STEM
educators. ITEEA strengthens STEM education through leadership, professional
development, membership services, publications, and relevant classroom activities
through the Engineering byDesign curriculum.

Publications

If you're interested in furthering your reading and want multiple resources that
cover both empirical studies and pro tips, I'd recommend you look into the following resources.

Books

- **ISTE Books (iste.org/learn/books).** ISTE is the among the leading publishers of
  books focused on technology in education. More than 80 titles focus on the
  most critical topics in edtech!

Magazine

- **Empowered Leader Magazine (iste.org/empowered-learner-magazine).** Print and
  online publication aimed at giving a voice to ISTE members and leaders in edtech.

Academic Journals

- **Journal of Research on Technology in Education (iste.org/jrte).** The *Journal of
  Research on Technology in Education* (*JRTE*) publishes articles that report on
  original research, project descriptions/evaluations, syntheses of the literature,
  assessments of the state of the art, and theoretical or conceptual positions
  that relate to the field of educational technology in teaching and learning and
  inform P–16 school-based practice.

- **Journal of Digital Learning in Teacher Education (iste.org/jdlte).** The *Journal of
  Digital Learning in Teacher Education* (*JDLTE*) is a refereed journal published
  quarterly in partnership with the ISTE Professional Learning Network for
  Teacher Educators. *JDLTE* provides access to the growing body of research
  addressing the use of digital technologies in teacher education. Articles highlight contemporary trends and effective, creative and innovative uses of digital
  technologies that prepare preservice, inservice and teacher educators for teaching in technology-rich learning environments.

- **Journal of Computer Science Integration (inspire.redlands.edu/jcsi).** The *Journal of Computer Science Integration (JCSI)* is an open access, peer-reviewed journal, and is sponsored by the University of Redland's School of Education and Armacost Library. JCSI aims to publish high-quality papers with a specific focus on K12 Computer Science integration that are accessible and of interest to educators, researchers, and practitioners alike.

How-to Blogs

- **EdSurge (edsurge.com).** A leading education news organization reporting on the people, ideas and technologies that shape the future of learning.

- **Edutopia Blog (edutopia.org).** Ideas and content for transforming K–12 education so that all students can acquire and effectively apply the knowledge, attitudes, and skills necessary to thrive in their studies, careers, and adult lives.

- **Getting Smart Blog (gettingsmart.com).** Supports innovations in learning, education & technology.

- **Tech & Learning (techlearning.com).** Tech & Learning provides print and digital publications, websites, e-newsletters, and online and in-person events on factual and evaluative information on trends, products, and strategies to education leaders who purchase technology products in their districts and schools.

- **ISTE Blog (iste.org/explore).** Ideas, content and resources for leading-edge educators.

- **Medium Lifelong Learning Defined in Education (medium.com/lifelong-learning-defined).** How-to blogs by educational coach Jorge Valenzuela.

Podcasts

- **ISTE Podcast | Your Edtech Questions (info.iste.org/your-edtech-questions).** ISTE's podcast tackles critical questions at the juncture of edtech research and classroom practice. In each episode, Zac Chase and Amal Giknis turn your edtech questions into practical edtech answers with the help of an ISTE expert.

- **STEM Everyday Podcast – dailySTEM (dailystem.com/stem-everyday-podcast).** The STEM Everyday podcast is hosted by Chris Woods and focuses on how teachers can infuse STEM (science, technology, engineering, and mathematics) into their everyday lessons. Chris helps listeners explore and share great ideas that inspire students to take ownership in their learning. Each week he interviews educators who are using innovative ways to add STEM to their everyday classrooms, schools, and communities.

- **Teach Better Talk Podcast (teachbetter.com/podcast).** Featuring expert educators ready to share progressive tactics to reach more students, Teach Better Talk is created by teachers, and fueled by passion! Every week, Rae Hughart and Jeff Gargas, of the Teach Better Team and www.teachbetter.com, chat with educators from all around the world, discussing failures, successes, exciting new tactics, and dishing out loads of tips, tricks, and advice for educators of all levels.

- **Teachers on Fire Podcast (teachersonfire.net/about).** Teachers on Fire podcast host Tim Cavey profiles agents of growth and transformation in K-12 education. Each week, he chats with an inspiring educator to bring you their highs and lows, passions and goals, and the voices and influences that are shaping their thinking and inspiring their practice.

- **TNT Edtech Podcast (sites.google.com/view/tntedtech).** Join Scott Nunes and Matthew Ketchum as they explore edtech in this dynamic podcast featuring top educators with pro tips on using edtech!

- **Project Based Learning In Practice (apple.co/2MzFzcc).** Weekly tips, interviews, strategies and best practices in implementing Project Based Learning from instructional coach Shayla Adams-Stafford.

- **10 Minute Teacher Podcast (10minuteteacher.libsyn.com).** Every weekday, join full-time teacher Vicki Davis author of the Cool Cat Teacher Blog as she dives into what matters most to classroom teachers. The 10 Minute Teacher is your ten minute PD breakaway! The best and brightest educators and idea creators from around the world will inspire you as they are interviewed on this show.

ISTE Standards for Students

Today's students must be prepared to thrive in a constantly evolving technological landscape. The ISTE Standards for Students are designed to empower student voice and ensure that learning is a student-driven process.

1. Empowered Learner

Students leverage technology to take an active role in choosing, achieving and demonstrating competency in their learning goals, informed by the learning sciences.

a. Students articulate and set personal learning goals, develop strategies leveraging technology to achieve them and reflect on the learning process itself to improve learning outcomes.

b. Students build networks and customize their learning environments in ways that support the learning process.

c. Students use technology to seek feedback that informs and improves their practice and to demonstrate their learning in a variety of ways.

d. Students understand the fundamental concepts of technology operations, demonstrate the ability to choose, use and troubleshoot current technologies and are able to transfer their knowledge to explore emerging technologies.

2. Digital Citizen

Students recognize the rights, responsibilities and opportunities of living, learning and working in an interconnected digital world, and they act and model in ways that are safe, legal and ethical.

a. Students cultivate and manage their digital identity and reputation and are aware of the permanence of their actions in the digital world.

b. Students engage in positive, safe, legal and ethical behavior when using technology, including social interactions online or when using networked devices.

c. Students demonstrate an understanding of and respect for the rights and obligations of using and sharing intellectual property.

d. Students manage their personal data to maintain digital privacy and security and are aware of data-collection technology used to track their navigation online.

3. Knowledge Constructor

Students critically curate a variety of resources using digital tools to construct knowledge, produce creative artifacts and make meaningful learning experiences for themselves and others.

a. Students plan and employ effective research strategies to locate information and other resources for their intellectual or creative pursuits.

b. Students evaluate the accuracy, perspective, credibility and relevance of information, media, data or other resources.

c. Students curate information from digital resources using a variety of tools and methods to create collections of artifacts that demonstrate meaningful connections or conclusions.

d. Students build knowledge by actively exploring real-world issues and problems, developing ideas and theories and pursuing answers and solutions.

4. Innovative Designer

Students use a variety of technologies within a design process to identify and solve problems by creating new, useful or imaginative solutions.

a. Students know and use a deliberate design process for generating ideas, testing theories, creating innovative artifacts or solving authentic problems.

b. Students select and use digital tools to plan and manage a design process that considers design constraints and calculated risks.

c. Students develop, test and refine prototypes as part of a cyclical design process.

d. Students exhibit a tolerance for ambiguity, perseverance and the capacity to work with open-ended problems.

5. Computational Thinker

Students develop and employ strategies for understanding and solving problems in ways that leverage the power of technological methods to develop and test solutions.

a. Students formulate problem definitions suited for technology-assisted methods such as data analysis, abstract models and algorithmic thinking in exploring and finding solutions.

b. Students collect data or identify relevant data sets, use digital tools to analyze them, and represent data in various ways to facilitate problem-solving and decision-making.

c. Students break problems into component parts, extract key information, and develop descriptive models to understand complex systems or facilitate problem-solving.

d. Students understand how automation works and use algorithmic thinking to develop a sequence of steps to create and test automated solutions.

6. Creative Communicator

Students communicate clearly and express themselves creatively for a variety of purposes using the platforms, tools, styles, formats and digital media appropriate to their goals.

a. Students choose the appropriate platforms and tools for meeting the desired objectives of their creation or communication.

b. Students create original works or responsibly repurpose or remix digital resources into new creations.

c. Students communicate complex ideas clearly and effectively by creating or using a variety of digital objects such as visualizations, models or simulations.

d. Students publish or present content that customizes the message and medium for their intended audiences.

7. Global Collaborator

Students use digital tools to broaden their perspectives and enrich their learning by collaborating with others and working effectively in teams locally and globally.

a. Students use digital tools to connect with learners from a variety of backgrounds and cultures, engaging with them in ways that broaden mutual understanding and learning.

b. Students use collaborative technologies to work with others, including peers, experts or community members, to examine issues and problems from multiple viewpoints.

c. Students contribute constructively to project teams, assuming various roles and responsibilities to work effectively toward a common goal.

d. Students explore local and global issues and use collaborative technologies to work with others to investigate solutions.

References

Banilower, E. R., Smith, P. S., Weiss, I. R., Malzahn, K. A., Campbell, K. M., & Weis, A. M. (2013). Report of the 2012 National Survey of Science and Mathematics Education. Chapel Hill, NC: Horizon Research, Inc.

Boyes, K., & Watts, G., (2009). Developing habits of mind in elementary schools: An ASCD action tool. Retrieved on http://www.ascd.org/Publications/Books/

Overview/Developing-Habits-of-Mind-in-Elementary-Schools.aspx

Center for Public Education, (2016). Educational equity: What does it mean? How do we know when we reach it? Retrieved on http://www.centerforpubliceducation.org/system/files/Equity%20Symposium_0.pdf

Core State Standards Initiative, (2019). Standards for mathematical practice. Retrieved on http://www.corestandards.org/Math/Practice/

Dorph, R., Shields, P., Tiffany-Morales, J., Hartry, A., McCaffrey, T. (2011). High hopes–few opportunities: The status of elementary science education in California. Sacramento, CA: The Center for the Future of Teaching and Learning at WestEd.

Edtech Teacher. (2018). Who we are: Edtech Teacher. Retrieved on https://edtechteacher.org/about/

Hilliard, P., (2015). Performance-based assessment: Reviewing the basics. Retrieved on https://www.edutopia.org/blog/performance-based-assessment-reviewing-basics-patricia-hilliard

Groome, M., (2017). Op-Ed: Is the investment in STEM education paying off? Retrieved on https://www.usnews.com/news/stem-solutions/articles/2017-08-17/op-ed-is-the-investment-in-stem-education-paying-off

Guzdial, M., (2015). *Learner-centered design of computing education: Research on computing for everyone, ser. synthesis lectures on human-centered informatics.* San Rafael, CA: Morgan & Claypool.

ISTE, (2019). Professional learning networks. Retrieved on http://community.iste.org/community/learningnetworks?_ga=2.16494526.942910991.1529977989-837332603.1516026135&CLK=54ea47b1-73fa-4e22-a1f9-7afc96964b78

K-12 Computer Science Framework Steering Committee, (2016). K-12 Computer Science Framework. New York, NY (p. 1, 2, 13, 68, 157).

Llovio, L. (2016). Governor signs legislation to make computer science part of the SOL curriculum. Retrieved from http://www.richmond.com/news/local/education/ /districts/governor-signs-legislation-to-make-computer-science-part-of-sol/article_36fe1085-9da0-59f5-b3d0-732a5ada5eb1.html

Matson, B., (2018). Conquering the workshop: A step-by-step guide to implementing the math workshop model in your K-5 classroom. https://www.ace.edu/blog/post/2018/04/12/a-step-by-step-guide-to-implementing-the-math-workshop-model-in-your-k-5-classroom

National Council for the Social Studies (NCSS), (1992). National Council for the Social Studies, Expectations of Excellence: Curriculum Standards for Social Studies (Washington, D.C.: NCSS, 1994): 3.1

National Council for the Social Studies (NCSS), (2013). Technology position statement and guidelines: Revised and approved by NCSS Board of Directors 2013. Retrieved on https://www.socialstudies.org/positions/technology

National Council for the Social Studies (NCSS), (2019). College, career, and civic life (C3) framework for social studies state standards: Guidance for enhancing the rigor of K-12 civics, economics, geography, and history. Retrieved on https://www.socialstudies.org/c3

National Council of Teachers of English, (2013). The NCTE definition of 21st century literacies. Retrieved from http://www2.ncte.org/statement/21stcentdefinition/

National Research Council, (2007). Taking science to school: Learning and teaching science in grades K-8. Committee on Science Learning, Kindergarten Through Eighth Grade. R. A. Duschl, H. A. Schweingruber, & A. W. Shouse (Eds.), Board on Science Education, Center for Education. Division of Behavioral and Social

Sciences and Education. Washington, DC: The National Academies Press. Retrieved from http://www.nap.edu/catalog.php?record_id=11625

National Research Council, (2012). A Framework for K-12 Science Education: Practices, Crosscutting Concepts, and Core Ideas. Washington, DC: The National Academies Press (p. 65).

Next Generation Science Standards, (2019). Next Generation Science Standards: For states, by states. Retrieved from https://www.nextgenscience.org/

Papert, S. (1980). *Mindstorms: Children, computers and powerful ideas.* New York, NY: Basic Books.

Piaget, J. (1974). To Understand Is to Invent. N.Y.: Basic Books.

Rouse, M., (2015). Definition from WhatIs.com: Robotics. TechTarget Network. Retrieved from https://whatis.techtarget.com/definition/robotics

Sisman, B., & Kucuk, S. (2019). An educational robotics course: Examination of educational potentials and pre-service teachers experiences. International Journal of Research in Education and Science (IJRES), 5(2), 510-531.

Tucker, A., McCowan, D., Deek, F., Stephenson, C., Jones, J., & Verno, A., (2006). A model curriculum for K-12 computer science: Report of the CM K-12 task force curriculum committee (2nd ed.). New York, NY: Association for Computing Machinery (p. 2).

Valenzuela, J. (2019). Attitudes Towards Teaching Computational Thinking and Computer Science: Insights from Educator Interviews and Focus Groups. *Journal of Computer Science Integration, 2* (2).

Virginia Department of Education (2016). *VDOE: Graduation (Diploma) Seals of Achievement.* Retrieved from http://www.doe.virginia.gov/instruction/graduation/profile-grad/

U.S. Department of Education, (2016). Non-regulatory guidance student support and academic enrichment grants. Retrieved on https://www2.ed.gov/policy/elsec/leg/essa/essassaegrantguid10212016.pdf

Wing, J., (2006). Computational thinking. *Communications of the ACM, 49*(3), 33-35

Index

Bring Jorge Valenzuela to your school, university, or conference!

Jorge Valenzuela is an award-winning writer, published researcher, experienced teacher, talented keynote speaker, and exciting workshop facilitator. Jorge balances every learning experience with the most current and relevant research, personal experiences from the field, and opportunities for participants to engage, reflect, interact, and apply.

His popular speaking and workshop topics* include:

- Inspirational keynotes

- Project based learning

- Computational thinking implementation across the curriculum

- Coding and programming with littleBits and Sphero

- Curriculum development

- Engineering design implementation

- Practical tips for social and emotional learning

- Lifelong Learning Defined life class

* These topics, and many more, can all be personalized to fit your organization's needs.

Connect with him at **lifelonglearningdefined.com** or on Twitter and Instagram **@JorgeDoesPBL**.